C000240862

DEFENDING HER SON

Prose Series 51

Canadä

Guernica Editions Inc. acknowledges the financial support
of the Canada Council for the Arts.
Guernica Editions Inc. acknowledges the financial support
of the Ontario Arts Council.
Guernica Editions Inc. acknowledges the financial support
of the Government of Canada through the Book Publishing Industry
Development Program (BPIDP).

John O'Meara

Defending Her Son

A Memoir

Guernica
Toronto·Buffalo·Lancaster (U.K.)
2000

Copyright © 2000, by John O'Meara and Guernica Editions Inc.
All rights reserved. The use of any part of this publication, reproduced,
transmitted in any form or by any means, electronic, mechanical,
photocopying, recording or otherwise stored in a retrieval system, without
the prior consent of the publisher is an infringement of the copyright law.

Antonio D'Alfonso, editor
Guernica Editions Inc.
P.O. Box 117, Station P, Toronto (ON), Canada M5S 2S6
2250 Military Road, Tonawanda, N.Y. 14150-6000 U.S.A.
Gazelle, Falcon House, Queen Square, Lancaster LA1 1RN U.K.

Typeset by Selina.
Printed in Canada.

Legal Deposit — First Quarter
National Library of Canada
Library of Congress Catalog Card Number: 00-100880
Canadian Cataloguing in Publication Data
O'Meara, John
Defending her son
(Prose series ; 51)
ISBN 1-55071-105-9
1. Critics–Canada–Biography.
2. Anthroposophists–Canada–Biography.
I. Title. II. Series.
PR2972.O64A3 2000   801'.95'092   C00-900189-1

For Antonio D'Alfonso,
most faithful of literary friends

Those cultures that are being cross-cultured, transcultured, are expected to be strong cultures. Whereas I am saying that a culture that is *debole,* that has faded, is the most interesting in possibilities . . . That is, all culture is basically an impermanent mutation. Culture, to be vital, should be in a weakened position.

Antonio D'Alfonso,
Duologue: On Culture and Identity

PREFACE

I take the title for this short record of my life from a phrase by
John Milton from the opening of Book VII of *Paradise Lost*.
Milton at this point speaks of the success he is counting on in
his imagination of otherworlds far removed from our own
world, and he contrasts his prospective achievement with the
tragic failure of Orpheus, who himself succeeds in going
down into Hell to bring up his dead wife, Eurydice, but who
must lose her on his return when, disobeying the injunction
of the lower gods not to do so, he looks back to see if she is
indeed come up with him. With that gesture of Orpheus',
Eurydice falls back into Hell, and as the story relates, Orpheus
is later dismembered by a troop of frenzied Bacchanalian
women who resent his spiritual-artistic independence from
their kind.

On one point the reader of my life will have to be
disappointed: the women around whom in a sense this life is
constructed have nothing in common with the frenzied kind
— for all were fine, upstanding women. However, it remains
true that, although they have in every case been indispensable in the evolution of my life, these women become associated in my mind at a certain point with an effect of arrest and
even with the prospect of my oblivion. Calliope, who was
Orpheus' Muse and also his mother, was in the end unable to
"defend" her son from his own destruction and death. Clearly
I cannot claim to be any Orpheus myself, but my own intellectual development, as reflected in the books I have written,
may certainly be said to be *after* the Orphic pattern — in
respect of the desire I show to penetrate the relationship

between death and otherworlds. This development was, to an extent, refracted out of the very pattern of my life. My devotion to a certain course of spiritual-intellectual development in my own life would lead me repeatedly to resist my associations with the women who seemed to be heralding in and helping to shape that very development. It had always seemed, in fact, that my choice of having such associations at all was wrong from the start — in relation, that is, to the deeper development that seemed designed for me. On the other hand, it has been the hardest thing in the world to resist or to be forced to resist these associations, with the consequence that, in clinging to them, I seemed continually faced with the prospect of oblivion both in spiritual and intellectual terms. At the same time, there were the many prospects of hard death I faced from the many separations that followed as a matter of course — separations made all the harder by the special meaning I had formerly attached to these associations. U*n-like* in the case of Orpheus, however, I have been *repeatedly* defended from death in the many forms that I have faced: the *difference* with Orpheus seemed to me worth highlighting, and so *my* positive use of Milton's negative reference in my title. Over time it became clear to me who my ever-elusive Eurydice was, on behalf of whom I would need so much defending and have to pass through so much. However, to this day I am unable to say who that Calliope has been who has watched over me so jealously from the first.

It may be that deep down all men are Orpheuses and that we all have our vigilant and demanding Calliopes seeing us through the (sometimes frightening) complexity of our lives. Certainly we are all put through our instruction in the ways of nature, intellect and art, from the very time we are born and grow up under the guidance of this mentor or the other. All would seem to be offered the specific nurturing intended for them (or should have been), and it may also be that each one of us is given his or her specific instruction and specific task to command. A solitude which I have always felt was intended to be peaceful but which, because of my embroilment, turned out always to be distressing has played a very large part in my own life. I would not be able to say just how solitary it has seemed to me to be. The task that was set me seemed to call for my coping very largely on my own, except, of course, for the incidental help of some good friends and the gift of inheritance from my very great ancestors — notably my great-grandparents, who bore more in the quality of their blood and in the conduct of their lives than I feel I deserved to inherit.

This is no story of success — as in the perfect rigor of Milton's own devotion to *his* task. Although *all* of the life that I recount here has been indispensable paradoxically to the task that was set me, the life I finally present is, tragically, one of enforced disassociation after enforced disassociation — to what end I speculate upon in these pages. The pattern is constant, except, that is, for the very last in this succession. This is she who brought the hope that in the story of my life some significant perception of the powers that go into making lives might be had for others — she who is my Nausicaa, my Pallas Athena, and my Penelope all in one, and to whom the life about which I write here finally leads me. *Around her* the story of my life — as a struggling Orpheus — is suddenly changed, into another that in the end involves me in a re-writing of the one I must offer the reader first.

I

It was in the spring I was born that my father finally succeeded in buying our glorious country-place in the sedate
Laurentian hills of Quebec province — that inestimable country-place that was to become our family treasure, and my
own. It was daring of my father at the time, for he now had
three children, and although, as a dispensing optician, he
managed a fairly well-paying job, he had had to borrow a
good deal of the five hundred dollars that he needed, turning
for the last portion of that required sum to his maternal
grandfather — Pe-Père Lavigne. It seems fitting that Pe-Père
should have been the one who finally made the purchase
possible, since it was he who bore our American-Indian blood
into the family, although he himself, in the five years he had
to live, did not visit the place, never leaving the solitary life he
maintained in the city in a room with my father's parents.

It is to the back veranda of our countryplace on the side
of the lake, no doubt in the summer of that year, that I can
trace my very oldest memory. One early summer morning it
would have been just warm enough for my mother to take me
out onto that veranda, and while I fed placidly, I should have
heard the sharp singular calls of the crows punctuating the
almost perfect silence of that time and place. Many other
species of bird were also out and about, though none of their
sounds would have penetrated to me the way the sound of
the crows did. When, many years later, I came to realize the
haunting influence the crow's call has on me, I observed that
the crow is a bird that *seeks out* quiet times and spaces; its
presence and call have often marked those quietest times and

places when I have been most deeply in touch with myself and very often alone, though I often did not anticipate the condition at the time.

At a certain point, the call of the crow would have gotten inextricably associated in my mind with the lake whose influence and effect I must already have sensed as I fed during those first months — since everyone and everything is changed in the presence of a lake. My mother's own fondest memories of the place were of the strong, wonderful shimmering cast by the sun across the water in the early morning from the other shore. I myself remember, most vividly of all, those mornings when, as a young boy, I left the dark, sometimes slightly damp, interior of the house by the front door, turning down the corner of the house on the right to be met at once by the strong glimmering of the water and the powerful warmth of the sun in which I chose to bask for an interval. By this time, the grove of pine trees that my Irish grandfather had planted around the house that first summer had ascended to a good height — those trees which were to tower so splendidly later giving the feeling of being on an estate, while beyond them the view of the lake was unobstructed, the land behind the house suddenly falling flat almost to lake level. In those early years, that land was covered with its own dense woods, until much cutting and weeding over many summers (by my grandfather originally) had left the land quite bare, except for a couple of spruce trees, which I remember being very old and hoary, one of these almost growing into the lake. That bottom land remained, in spite of these intense efforts of cultivation, almost always wet, the water rising in the spring right up to that mild, fortunate slope that kept the house always safely removed from the deluge.

The lake itself was full of weeds at the shore line and gave the impression of a place that would only get colder and murkier towards its center. It was said that the lake was named after a man who had drowned in it and was never recovered — Lake Ménard it was. Despite the eerie legend, which never really reached our family consciousness, the lake always made an impression of sublime placidness. It was just large enough to give the feeling of some vastness, yet small enough to inspire the feeling that one might just walk across to its other side. Its constant and inexhaustible life (undisturbed over ages) was perhaps the only actual experience of the eternal I have ever had, when I had the habit (by then a young student of literature) of lingering for periods of time by its shores. The feeling of an eternal presence and life would continue into the evening when, with the fall of dusk and the creeping shadows, frogs and birds concentrated themselves in a great litany of nightly farewell, and the lake, now that darkness had fallen, went into its own dark sleep that only seemed another awakening.

*

In one of the earliest photographs of me that survive, I am sitting, at the age of three, on a good-sized rock that had been left in front of the house when the land was originally cleared. I am clasping our family dog tightly to me as if affirming my right to the possession of it. No doubt, my father would have been telling me to hold on tightly, because he wanted to get the dog along with me into the photograph. That rock was to be in the many years to come the site of almost every photograph that was ever taken of anyone who came to the place. I doubt, however, that anyone over that time ever gave much thought to how old that rock was, lying there as a member of the Laurentian shield — one of the oldest in the world. There were, of course, many of these age-old rocks, of greater or lesser size, lying open to view in every region of the area.

The rock that stood in front of our house was left bare, as in the photograph, for some time, until one day someone had the fancy idea of painting the rock white to go with the wooden frame around the house that had in the meantime also been painted white. From the lake our land rolled slowly up a low, finely graded hill that was cut across about half way up by the village road. Those far ends marked the extremities of our land, with the house lying just about half way in between. The road itself led onwards into the village to the north east where it came to an end at the village church — from here, one turned either left or right, depending on whether one was going east or northwest. The church itself could be seen from almost every point around the lake. In those days fences stood to mark the boundaries of the various properties and were never meant to keep people out, since one could always easily climb them or get under them, and in this way, as children, myself and my younger brother got to scout out — to see and to feel — almost every inch of country space there was in the area, both around and beyond the lake, in entire freedom and without fear of recriminating proprietors. Climbing and carving birch trees in some faraway woods, like our own Indian ancestors, while imagining we actually lived in those woods for a time — this got to be among our favorite and most endearing pastimes.

In spite of the great peace and beauty of the new place — as I like to imagine, especially in those early morning hours — those first few months after my birth must have been very hard for my mother. For with my own birth, my mother had lost my twin sister, who was born dead. My mother tells me that she lavished a double tenderness and care on me in consequence, appalled that I too might have died. And so, my growing up in these first months was imbued from the start with an atmosphere of death and some sorrow, countered by an increase of love. In the last month of my mother's preg-

nancy, I lay in a womb that had already turned into a grave
on one side, and for some time there had been some fear for
my mother when she had started to become ill from the
burden of the death: it was never known until she delivered.
Only my father, with his characteristic insistence on knowing
all that was rightly his, actually got to see my twin who must
then have been a shrivelled corpse. His own grandmother, on
his mother's side, had been ill herself over this time; it was
known that Me-mère was on her deathbed, and when she
heard of the young death, she is remembered to have said that
she wished that God might have taken her instead. Me-mère
died within five days of my own birth.

My recollections of Pe-Père are peculiar, for I have no
memory of his face, or any other part of him except for a huge
knee as he sat on his bed in that small room while I idled about
him, struck by the strong smell of his pipe-smoking which
must have been rank, though to my young self it only had the
fascination of what defined him uniquely from the rest of the
family. I distinctly remember to this day walking up that
closed flight of inner stairs to get to my grandparents' third
storey flat on Papineau Street, thinking to myself, as I took the
last turning up, that it was there, behind the ventilator screen,
that Pe-Père's room lay, with that distinctive smell of his
pipe-smoking which was his life to me. My father, over the
course of his own life — perhaps struck more and more with
the thought that he too would soon be aging — would often
return to the way my great-grandfather had spent his last
years, appalled that he had been allowed to stay pent up there
— a complete recluse. But Pe-Père must have been gladdened
to receive the regular visits of his small great-grandchildren
who by then were growing fast in numbers, and he is remembered as a great tease — a broad-built, huge man with very
much the look of the strong, hard-working farmer that he had
been, who had had the other remembered quality of passing

on his singularly large ears to the next generations (and so to my father). Though I was five when he died, I have no memory whatever of his death or any experience of the bereavement that would have accompanied it: and to me he seemed never to have died at all.

My earliest vivid memories in childhood are not of the country place that was to loom large in my life and imagination; they belong rather to my first time spent in our third storey apartment on Castelneau Street. These are of the sparrows that would alight for brief moments on the cement window-sills that still showed the sparkle of their sand grains, while I watched the birds from up close — so very close, it seemed to me then — across the glass window that had been opened only slightly to let in the fresh air and life of that outer space. That sensual body of free animal life, so close to my touch and possession in those moments, thrilled me with the strangest delight and warmth, and it is with the same rich feeling of sensual unity with those free, bodied creatures that I used, at a later age, to gloat over my conquest of the stray alley cat that I had had the easy ability to attract to my arms. On those occasions, I used to take the cat home, up the flight of inner stairs, to my mother, who was all too ready to satisfy my wish that the cat be offered some milk to drink out of a saucer, while the cat fed freely on the outer landing, quite at ease and unmenaced. It was with the same awe of sensual life that I used invariably, while the cat was feeding, to dunk the tip of its nose and whiskers into the soft milk, to have the rich impression that made.

It is a touching wonder to me how readily a mother will satisfy her young child's delight without questioning or remonstrating, though my mother had perhaps too much of our family sense of trusting liberty, for I cannot think how I myself would trust my own children to the freedom of the street at so young an age. I was not supervised while I took to the streets — I must have been four or five; and there *was* an almost fatal incident. I had, quite unthinkingly, run across Berri Street after a ball that had gotten away from a group of us children, turning to recross the street, also without any thought. To the great distress of a motorist who had begun to sound his horn while I was re-crossing, a cyclist was blocking his way at this very moment. To this guardian angel, then, or rather to his messenger, I owed my life: it was to be the first of two incidents in my life when I was saved from calamity, apart from the circumstances of my birth. But I did not come away from the street in this instance without being run over by the cyclist himself.

While most other children would no doubt have looked to their mothers for pity and relief from a vicious stroke of fate, what I felt was guilt, and it took some courage on my part to report the event to my mother. I was bruised and scarred from the violent hit, but as the accident had involved a cyclist who did not feel the event had to be reported (I suppose since it also involved an unknowing child of four or five), I myself could get away with reporting very simply that I had been hit by a bicycle. My mother never learned how close I had come to death once again. On the other hand, I certainly retained a vivid memory of the event, so that when my best friend down the street was, at a later time, hit by a car himself, though he was not critically injured, I had no trouble experiencing the graveness of the moment. Our family (my mother was there certainly) watched the event unravel from the balcony of our third-storey apartment. It is, among other things, curious that as a child, even so young, one can have that experience of the earthly terror of fatality (so preternaturally physical in the case of a car accident). One seems to have the experience in a far more intense way when young than at a later age.

My Irish grandfather had received the task of keeping both me and my younger brother when my mother went back to work for a time — he who had done the weeding on the lower land and had planted the pine trees that were to grow to such a proud height around our country home. But, in spite of that time spent largely with my grandfather, I have strangely very few memories of him, except for those times when I lay alongside him in bed and docilely scratched his head for what seemed like an eternity. From what was said about him later by the family and from pictures of him that survive, he must have been much like my father. There is a picture of them both — my father may have been in his mid-twenties at the time; my grandfather in his fifties — taking the full proud measure of each other with a perfectly poised handshake, full eyes dead square on each other, in a way that would only be thinkable within Irish culture. My grandfather was a man whose typical Irish pride of life I would have wished to satisfy — being that kind of child myself. Satisfying that pride also meant scratching his head without protest, till his scalp would come off in scales in my tender hands. One thing I do remember about my grandfather, however, was the morning of his death. It was the first time a death had been announced to me, or at least the first time I remember it being announced. My mother was home that morning, sitting in quiet pain at the kitchen table, and, sensing the sadness of the occasion, I was making my own bed (for what I think was my first time) when my father entered the apartment. When he came into my room, I was so struck by his pain — the first time I had ever witnessed pain in my father — that I instinctively walked right up to him, burying my head in his lap in a completely shared sorrow. He had not yet turned forty; the blow had pierced through him like a sword, and he would never be the same again. A new bitterness would infest his soul by slow degrees, though it would not break out — or at least I did not become finally

conscious of it — until some few years later when much
trouble broke out between himself and my elder brother.

It was in the winter of that same year that I broke my left
leg while at school. I was in the oldest group that occupied the
school's smaller recess-yard, and I had condescendingly
spread myself over a younger boy who had wilfully kicked
our ball down to the other end of the schoolyard — to school
him in decent behavior — when an entire gang of young
boys, inadvertently tussling amongst each other, fell squarely
onto my outstretched leg. I remember crying out so wildly
everyone knew at once that something grave had taken place.
The effect of a broken leg, I remember, was eerie — as if the
leg had spread itself out throughout the schoolyard, like some
great watery snake — I felt it was everywhere. I was then
carried on someone's back into the Principal's office where I
was stretched out on one of the desks there. Both my mother
and my father soon arrived — they had gotten away from
work so quickly, now that I think back — and I remember my
father speaking to me as if I had everything to proud of: it was
just like him to leave me with the impression that the whole
experience was as natural as could be. All this took place
before my grandfather died (he was to die in late spring, two
days before his birthday).

I was to spend a full month in traction in the hospital,
during which time I received a great pirate-and-ship set as a
gift for my pains from my mother, and I became lost in the
great sea-adventures I was now free to imagine with the kind
of abandon that could only come from my being out of school.
My mother's devotion was typical, for although she could not
make it to the hospital during the day (it was my paternal
grandmother who then filled in, on occasion), my mother
visited me every evening after work, rushing to me after a
quick supper at home, and twice a day on weekends. This was
the time I was also attended to by what seemed to me an

extraordinarily tender and beautiful nurse — the first time I was attended to so closely by a young adult woman, who compared with some of my teachers. It was also during this time that I made my first adult friend of a male attendant who had the task of getting me to wash up every day — a young man in his late twenties and of no great beauty — whom yet I remember with the greatest tenderness: Edgar Deprès. I had over this time gotten so close to him that one day, when I was transferred to another area of the hospital — the transfer was overseen by the nurse whom I loved, I broke down in tears before her when she set me into the bed, knowing that I would no longer be seeing Edgar every day. I had in this way experienced the pangs of love for the first time. How remarkable that Edgar should have visited me at my home later when I was let go. He left me a photograph of himself, among other things, and I never saw him again after that. My school teacher at the time also visited me at my home (I had been her star student), and that too had been extraordinary — to have her, a fairly young woman still — into our very home. I was on crutches for a while, and not always so very adept in the house, so that I sometimes tripped over myself, and I remember one occasion in particular when I did so, pleading with my elder brother (I think it was) not to mention the incident to my father whose pride I thought I might have offended in falling.

My father had gotten our country home, he often reminded us, to get his children off the streets in the summer, but of course that meant that he would stay behind in the city to work, leaving my mother to fend for herself with four children. It took some courage for my mother to be up in the country, because of the deep blackness of night in those days, before electricity came to the roads and spotlights came into fashion. My mother would have to abide those dark times alone with her four children in a house that was exposed to intruders — though for this reason we had the dog. In spite of

this, I never as a child felt fear, nor was there ever any incident. I never imagined fear and felt otherwise always pro-
tected. The most trying moments were the great thunder-
storms, which would invariably wake us in the middle of the
night. All the children slept on the upper storey of the house,
which was barely finished—there was nothing to protect us
from the large nails that obtruded from the roofing right
above our heads as we lay in bed, so that we had carefully to
avoid sleeping too close to the outer edges of the slanting roof.
It was easy to feel that the bellowing storm was just the other
side of the roof: the noise was quite deafening, not to mention
the great flashes of light. Yet as the second boy, I had the
advantage, during those nights of storm, of sleeping right up
against my older brother who did not seem himself disturbed
(being seven years my senior), and he seemed to me, on those
occasions, to be all the defense I needed.

Among my mother's many civilized habits while we
were in the country (they prevailed in spite of the darkness
and the fear in her) by far the most beautiful was the one she
had on the Friday evening that heralded in my father's re-appearance. My father used to work till nine at night, so that he
could not possibly make it up to the country house until well
after eleven. In spite of this, my mother would always arrange
to free herself early that particular evening, so that she could
assume her place at the far-end of the back veranda, which in
those days had screens, looking towards the road. From here,
she would supervise the appearance of every car that came
over the hill from the left towards the house, from that early
time in the evening until darkness descended when, to the
sound of every appearing car — which was very distinctly
heard in that quiet country — were now added the searching
beamlights. She would in this way attend on the appearance
of a good many cars, each of which heralded in the one she
waited for — until it became clear that it was he who *had*

arrived, for this car would suddenly slow down, and the beamlights would take a sharp turn downwards, as my father veered into the gravel path that led towards the house.

That is how I saw it at a later age, for in the early days we children would be asleep. But it was our custom to insist to our mother that we be awakened when our father did arrive — it was his unchanging habit to ascend to our upper storey to wake us up himself, for it must have been a great pleasure for my father also to be with his own again.The moment remains among the most magical from my young childhood. It was his custom on these occasions to kiss us squarely on the mouth, boys and girl alike; there could be no failure of affection, or squeamishness, in my father to whom, one felt, we were everything. There was general rejoicing from that moment as we all took our place downstairs, basking in the magic of my father's return and the pleasure of the few treats we were entitled to have, which he had brought with him. All darkness was then dispelled. Only later, of course, did I come to understand and appreciate why my mother would be in bed so much later the following morning. My father would make it his own task to get up in those very cold hours of the early morning, to get the woodstove going; on every other day during the week, we gave, of course, no thought to this function, getting up to a downstairs area that was always already warm when we came down.

II

Primarily, I was greatly marked by my Catholic upbringing while at school. There was the usual First Communion, of course. Only I seemed to have taken the idea of being wedded to my female partner quite as seriously as I did the Communion itself. She would mark me for some time to come, Louise; she would remain — a magical presence to me there on the other side of our segregated school, to be seen, though always at a distance, in the large schoolyard during recess. Word of my attraction to her got around among chums, and on one occasion — it was a late spring evening — for some reason she was still at school, playing in a now unsupervised schoolyard (our family lived just across from the school, so I often got to play there myself). There had been a disruption in our respective games, and she and I found ourselves dispersed and suddenly out of each other's sight — for the secret of my attraction to her had been let out of the bag! I remember running away from my friends around the corner of the school in boyish embarrassment only to meet up directly with her, who had learned of my spilled out feelings. Nothing can express the magic and charm of discovering in that priceless moment, though nothing whatever was said between us (not ridicule, as I might have expected, but rather) her own obviously intense pleasure at what I felt about her.

Who can express the power or significance of those first emanations of love, though nothing else came of it? The encounter alone of two young children in complete freedom and innocence, in the fine, warm air of late spring: strange to say, those feelings and that encounter were in my case inseparable from religion. In the same school year that I broke my leg and my grandfather died, I had joined, of my own initiative, the school's church choir: the Holy Family Boys' Choir, as it was then called. I was to remain in that choir for a good seven years, till I turned fourteen. We still sang the Mass in Latin in those days — a High Mass every Sunday, singing also on special occasions, ordinations among others, for we had become one of the most reputable liturgical choirs in the Catholic diocese. Who can say what sense of order was brought into our souls by this constant practice and discipline in good singing at this level, in an ancient spiritual language — not to mention our sharing in the Eucharist from week to week? An astonishing potential for sensitivity was created that sometimes came to a head, as I recall in the case of the last Corpus Christi celebration held while I was still in grade school (I was twelve, by then).

We took to the streets in procession in those days — the event coincided with the celebration of Midsummer (towards the end of June) — singing the "Tantum Ergo" among other things, as the Church Monstrance (that ancient symbol of Christ as Cosmic Sun) was borne aloft and carried all through the church neighborhood. The event, I realize now, had something to do with experiencing the Body of Christ all around us in Its yearly Reunion with the outer Cosmos, and it got associated on that last occasion with another remarkable encounter whose magic and warmth I remember to this day. It happened just outside the schoolyard, on the girls' side, under that one, great oak tree that overspread the yard from the street. To think alone of how that tree had overseen so much over those many mornings and afternoons of our long apprenticeship there!

I was late for the event — all the others had already made their way to the church from the school where all had at first gathered. Alone, I found there, likewise late, my first girlfriend's companion, who was also alone and whom I remembered well from that First Communion several years before, as well as over the intervening years (she was Italian). She was standing there as if waiting for me, in a lilac dress, in the caressing warmth of that evening air, her dark-black hair crowned for the event with the customary flowers of midsummer, her dark-black eyes wondering at me for being late myself. I remember only some vague, embarrassed words that all the others had gone ahead and we would now have to join up with them quickly, though we walked over at our separate paces and along separate ways. I would see her only once more in later life, while we attended separate universities, on the street — I noted well that it was she, a habit of identification that I have always had — astonished that it *was* she, but I would not stop to speak to her.

Only one other moment out of my childhood compares in power to that final farewell encounter. It concerns the one who was my first actual girlfriend, when I had turned ten, my parents having moved to a larger, ground-floor house on St. Denis Street. The larger space meant we could allow ourselves the sort of dog my father always wanted — a Scottish collie, and it was I who was often given the task of walking it. On one such walk, the occasion was provided that allowed a young girl of about my age, who had greatly struck me, to address me. Josée was her name — with long, honey-blond hair. We had often walked past each other on our separate ways home from school — she returning from her French school from the South, I from my English school from the North. Again, it seemed there was no one on the streets but ourselves. She had gotten mixed up in my mind with the image of the girl from the Fatima story that I had learned about, and partly I was enamored from the story, though the actuality of meeting Josée had more than enough power of its own. I was eventually invited up by her to their family resi-

dence (a second-floor dwelling) into what seemed to me like
an inner sanctum. It was the first time I had ever penetrated
the space of strangers under such circumstances — the very
texture of the air seemed to announce their most intimate
sensibilities to me. The father (a History teacher) was reading
in his office at the entrance to the house; the mother was very
welcoming and herself impressed with the moment, which
she seemed to regard with a satisfaction of her own — well
aware of what it meant that her daughter had taken to me.

There was a perfect mannerliness and a perfectly
charmed freedom about the mother, as I recall, as she left us
to entertain ourselves in the company of Josée's slightly
younger sister. We sat on one of the beds in their bedroom
and played cards, while every so often, as the cards were
being raked and shuffled, Josée took my hand. Almost every
afternoon after school Josée would be let out later than I was,
and I would be sitting at my father's work table (he had built
up a small home business, and he had an office in the front of
the house). I would be doing my homework lessons, my back
turned to the window and the street, but always anticipating
that moment when Josée would finally come by and, from the
sidewalk by the house gates, call out my name — to announce
herself and to greet me. Nothing more was said; she went on
her way — but for the warmth and perfection of that ritual,
very little has compared since. It is invariably some warm
season that comes to mind when I think back to that ritual —
some point in late spring on approaching summer — though
the season may well have been winter. How strange to think
back to Josée walking by me on that same sidewalk some
years later (we were in our late teens by then) now in the
company of another — the boyfriend she had made in the
meantime, strange that it should all have seemed so natural
for us to be growing up quite separately, as our fates had
ordained — she who had once offered me among the purest,

most complete moments from childhood. There was neither jealousy nor resentment between us, only a continued shared good feeling whenever we crossed each other's path, and an undying knowledge of our attachment once, which nothing and no one would replace.

*

My childhood had been spent primarily among family relations which were either Irish from my father's side, or Quebecois from my mother's. Being among those who vowed by a bilingual Canada, my Irish grandfather accordingly took the proud decision to send his children to French school, while English was spoken at home. There could be no more peculiar spectacle than my father gathering with his brothers and sister in later life, when I was old enough to notice how strange this was — my grandfather had died by then — all fiercely Irish in their pride and loud manners, all speaking French among themselves. My Quebecois mother, who had learned English from the time of her association with my father's family (at sixteen), by the time she had her own children had heard quite enough of my father's hard time at school, where he had been constantly teased about his Irish name. Much of that time my father had spent getting into scraps, and it was while at school that my father learned a habit of pugilism that never left him. It was an expression of his fearless nature, and on one occasion, so the story goes, my father had taken on a professional boxer who had been bullying my father's younger brother on the street: my father acquitted himself far better, it seems, than the boxer had imagined he would. I am also told that my father and grandfather on occasion took to fisticuffs themselves to settle matters between them — in old-world, Irish style. Horrified by my father's hard time while at school (and the example, I suspect, of my father's family), my mother reversed the pattern and sent us all to English school — however, with the approval, it would seem, of my father, who always projected a different set of manners for his children. Our parents developed the rather peculiar habit of always addressing us in English, though they always spoke French between themselves; in spite of this, we would be certain to learn French well enough, not only from my father's side of the family, but of course also from my mother's side.

Here all was mannerliness and seemingly inexhaustible affection: quite the best of mannerly, sentimental Quebec. The contrast between families was more than remarkable. On my mother's side were five sisters, each of whom could lavish more affection than the other on their more than treasured nephews and nieces. There was always great charm, and wonderful feasting and treating at Christmas and Easter especially, when all families on my mother's side got together. Here it was impossible not to feel provided for as in Heaven itself. On my father's side, by contrast, all was great (and very loud) good cheer, especially on New Year's Eve. Here was the Irish group-soul still fully alive — all aunts and uncles and spouses, nephews and nieces and cousins being one indivisible and impregnable family. Here it was quite impossible either to be unhappy, or ever to be alone. From my mother's family, I would learn too much mannerliness and sentiment for the world's ways; from my father's side too much fraternity and pride of character, also, too much robustness in the social life. The combination of these forces would make me in the end more inclined to strong, mannered action and to mannerliness than to conversation when in society, with the result that my social experience while I was growing up was never greatly satisfying — for it is the general understanding in society, of course, that there must be conversation from one — or else there is nothing.

One other consequence of growing up in such a tightly knit family, as my father's was, was that I made close friends of my cousins. I made a favorite of one while a child, spell-bound by his great fairness — he had sun-white blond hair — like my best (and only deep) friend at school — Norman — who was from a Scottish family, and with whom I shared a place at choir. When I was nearing adolescence, I made a favorite of another cousin for another reason: his deep, com-fortable silence, which always allowed me great freedom. He became my constant companion throughout the long sum-mer time when I turned twelve and thirteen (I had by then become a city person by choice). Among other things, we made the most of our time in another welcoming Quebecois household, when I in particular took a liking to a girl in his neighborhood — Nicole. Once again I was in the presence of a Quebecois mother who was more than happy to oblige the romance that had developed between us, though her daugh-ter was only ten. We sat regularly in their parlor, listening to records and occasionally dancing intimately to the softer songs, while Nicole's mother looked on approvingly from her privileged place in the living room armchair, reveling in her greatly treasured role as our benevolent chaperon.

III

For the most part, my childhood was marked by many relations of this sort, extended while in school and at church (while at choir) almost strictly to the Irish and Scottish people around me: I simply lived out what there was to be found as a dominant culture in the parish of Holy Family at that time. Yet I was well surrounded, already from early on, also by many Italians, both at school and at choir, though they seemed as yet not to have penetrated my consciousness in any pronounced way. However, when the time came to go to high school in St. Michel, the Italians had become the dominant culture, and I was greatly impressed by their intensely physical, sentient life, especially as I had started school a year early as a child, while many of these immigrant Italians had come into the system late without knowing the language. In some cases they were three or four years older, so that they appeared to me gigantic, both in size and manners. Fortunately, I was given the chance to make up for the deficiency in some way, when our gym teacher singled me out as the one whom he himself intended to mold into a gymnast.

He would often take special pride especially in later years in thinking and saying that I (the captain of the team by then) was the gymnast whom he had personally shaped, among all the others who had joined of their own volition. We turned out to be a championship team of gymnasts (in the circuit of Catholic schools — where everyone agreed to avoid the high bar), practising strenuously virtually every school day, in the morning before school, during lunch time and after school. Among the most memorable experiences over that time was the manner in which we got to competition. A team of six gymnasts, we were all squeezed in painfully (by his command) into our gym teacher's old Volkswagon beetle — myself, the smallest, on the passenger's knee in front — in the most illegal and foolhardy fashion. We set off, not without much daredevilry in our attitudes, which carried over into our performances. This was our youth! And there was the glamor of our being champions!

And it was while I was working at being a gymnast that I got to meet Liliana—herself a gymnast at school. The gym was for us, as was often the case in those days, the place where girls and boys could come about as close to each other as rules permitted. The long and very high folding door that separated both sides of the gym would on occasion be left open at the middle (by our more indulgent gym teachers), allowing those in training on each side a special view of the other sex in action. Everything seemed so easy then: as Liliana went by one day, running for warm-up, I simply addressed her; she stopped; we talked and, by the end of that conversation, we had arranged to go home together by bus. It was the beginning of a relationship that would last five years, certainly the most intense and among the most beautiful I have known.

Those first summers, I remained behind in the city — apart from my father who would come in late from work, I was the only one at home. It was the summer of the year I had graduated from high school; I was sixteen, Liliana fifteen; we had met in the spring of the previous year. Liliana would come to me every so often during the day, when she could manage to get away, for her very strict Italian father would never have allowed her out to see a boy. She would always arrange to go shopping with a girlfriend, using those occasions to get away. She would arrive — smelling sweetly from the warmth of the summer day, in a simple, cotton dress, often of dark-red color with flower designs, her long, dark-brown curly hair let down freely. She always seemed to carry herself like a gymnast. We had the whole house to ourselves and would spend hours in bed together, given up to a pure passionate love of each other which only intensified with time. Strangely enough, we never consummated that love, though it was as passionate as any I have ever read about.

That was also the summer I began my serious reading in literature: on days when I would not see Liliana, while at home alone I read a number of novels including: *Crime and Punishment, The Brothers Karamazov, The Grapes of Wrath.* Liliana and I continued altogether faithful to each other, though we could rarely meet. By then at college, I could only get to see her Friday afternoons when she would visit the house after school — on occasion my mother would be at home — and, far more rarely, on Saturdays over the winter. I would go down to see her in competition during her final year in high school. The following year, she went to college herself — a scholar at Marianopolis College where she specialized in French literature. She had been to grade school in French and, so, was fluent in three languages. Hers was the world of St. Exupery's *Little Prince,* though she too had become in the meantime a serious and successful scholar of literature.

I had had the idea, towards the end of my first year at college, of going away to work for the summer in the Canadian Rockies. How I could think of leaving Liliana that summer is beyond my comprehension today. I was to take up a job I had applied for at the Timberline Hotel in Banff, Alberta. What an impression was made on me when I stepped off the train in Banff that very first time (I had been confined to the train for almost three days) to find myself overpowered suddenly by the grandeur of those snow-capped mountains rising up all around on all four sides. Nothing like the gentle sloping hills of my childhood haven! There was also the very great freshness of the air unlike even what I had known at our country place. I took up residence in the staff lodgings just beside the hotel which was situated just above the trans-Can-ada highway. The view from the hotel took in the entire Banff Springs Valley with the great Bow River running through it — the Banff Springs Hotel rising from the center of the Valley, some distance away, like some great castle tower. I would make several forays into that valley, using one of the roads that wound its way into it, both on foot and on bicycle and on one occasion, quite freely, on horseback with a friend from the hotel who knew her own way around the valley, for she had been brought up in the area, and she rode her own horse, which she quite loved. To think that Liliana might have joined me there! We had, of course, the singular great pleasure of writing each other, and now could add to what we had shared some powerful dreaming about each other. Some of this I did at the time to the music of "Knights in White Satin," which I played repeatedly to myself, while thinking on her.

The Hotel had attracted some very remarkable transient souls. That first summer, I was lodged in the same room with an aspiring young painter (he must have been in his early twenties — David was his name). He had made a philosophy for himself out of some form of artistic rationalism that he had derived from two great composers: Beethoven and Stravin-sky. With him I listened carefully to Beethoven's late piano sonatas (the 101 and 111) as well as to *The Rite of Spring*. This was the first classical music I listened to, and I was more than impressed with the great rational confidence of this young man who struck me as a true artist. And indeed, his paintings (entirely of the mountainscapes around) had about them the very same uncompromising robustness (all in shades of grey; there was no color to them), the same Beethoven-like and Stravinsky-like rationality of form. I remember being greatly distressed when this rebellious and uncompromising young man simply left the hotel without warning (he had been the

Chef's aid) except for a short note (and a painting) he had left behind for me. He seemed to me some aspect of my own rebellious spirit that had awakened since my last year in high school. That summer I made the acquaintance also of Rick, a young philosopher graduate (very fond of Plato) who had just returned from a trip to India. He was himself in part East Indian, though Canadian-born; he seemed to me at the time to be not only the type but the model of a meditative mind — altogether the opposite of my painter-friend. How strange that these two should have converged in my own life! I had an extremely abstract mind at the time, living a little too purely (for this world) with my ideal "forms" (to invoke Plato) — the result, partly, of being so suddenly and intensely in love; so that the company of this meditative philosopher was very agreeable to me, while that of the painter represented more of a challenge to my awakening intellectuality, which I was in process of developing at college. These two were, indeed, like types of my own self, and the opposite of what one might expect (though this was the end of the 1960s): idealism in philosophy and rationality in art.

That year I had done extremely well in Social Philosophy (for college) and I had begun to be greatly roused by Literature. The works that have stuck in my mind — at opposite poles from each other — were *Darkness at Noon* and *A Separate Peace.* I had great capacity for reading structural patterning in literature, though my conceptual reasoning remained of course somewhat undeveloped. This will have nothing to do with the fact that I had been the top student in the sciences through all my high school years. I had also been top student in English, though there one received no training — all grades in English were significantly lower, and English had remained for me, as for everyone else, an obscure experience, impervious to rational scrutiny. In fact, only in my second year (of three) at university did the rational faculty

finally fully awaken with the full-scale tutoring that year of an
English professor who stood by logical structuring in literature (the best professor I had at University — Robert Philmus).
The awakening of conceptual capacity in youth remains, in
my view, one of the very greatest of mysteries.

I had also a wonderful social experience that summer,
for it was then that I made the acquaintance of André Cusson
— a Montrealer who had spent many years abroad in the rest
of Canada. He was considerably older than I was — thirty-
eight, as was his friend whom I also got to revere, himself also
a waiter at the hotel — Eric Davies. André had been in the
circuit of the more expensive clubs as a waiter over those years
and had followed the hotel manager to the Timberline from
one such club. In him I experienced a truly wonderful hauteur
of very great substance and dignity. None of this had left him
when I came across him more than twenty five years later.
André was both tall and very well-built, with a firm-set jaw
and a rugged-looking face that could yet show great tenderness and pride. He had a pride of character such as I had not
come across before, which only seemed the more outstanding
because it was so flexibly given to every one he served. It was
all the more extraordinary, then, to discover that he also had
a brute ego of great power, which he did not spare those
customers and any one else who offended his highly developed sense of civility and humanity. As he put it to me
himself: "Je peux aller du plus sublime au plus grotèsque!" A
very complex and powerful man, who was yet capable of
great selflessness: his giving — when he gave — was in
abundance, and it was entirely without thought of returns.

His associate and friend, Eric, whom he had accomo-
dated in his cabin in town, was Welsh, and himself a man of
very great poise and dignity. In him one felt there could be
nothing of the grotesque: of all those that I have met, certainly
the man of profoundest civility. He seemed to me then (and

seems to me now in my memory) the very model of self-con-
sciousness; I never knew him to have any flaws, he seemed to
be so well ahead of others in consciousness of any situation,
in respect of the way it reflected on human dignity. A tall
fair-haired man, balding, he seemed just in looking at one
from his heights to raise one up to a higher consciousness of
oneself. He had deliberately turned his back on a family
fortune in Wales to cultivate a life of simplicity and experience. André and Eric — both so utterly dissimilar, except in
their mutual love of human pride — these would be my
models of experience and of what I could expect to make of
myself in the power of human dignity.

I was to return to Banff for another two summers, André
remaining there throughout that time, while Eric had left, for
yet another set of adventures. Separating myself from Liliana
as I did in this way over three summers, our relationship had
grown somewhat strained, for, while I was venturing forth
into the world quite freely, she had remained house-bound
and had consequently grown more and more into her family's
social conventions. I was, at the same time, growing more and
more ambitious intellectually. I had taken a course on "Tragedy in the Western Tradition" which had transformed me,
and I was also devoting myself more and more to Shakespeare and quietly "living into" the circle of English at University.

Liliana, from the estrangement that had grown between
us, would fall into a serious depression that would, from time
to time, leave her mind blank, and for a period, she would
seek help from the outpatient clinic of a psychiatric institution
in Montreal. How sad this was my one great friend at the time
can say. Luigi Luzio had become my very close friend from
the time Liliana and I had first taken up, when I had conven-
iently introduced him to my Irish cousin, Christine. With her
I had retained a close attachment from the times when, still

grade-school children, we had had the habit of making our long way to school in the North of the city every morning and afternoon. Liliana and I, Christine and Luigi — we had become a close-knit foursome, all of us suddenly very intensely in love.

That period of time together had been marked by a very singular event: the Russian-made film of *War and Peace* had come out, directed by Sergei Bondarchuk. Liliana had been, until our growing estrangement, in her whole spirit and attitude, and even in her pure, simple style of dress, entirely of Natasha's nature, especially as played by the Russian actress in this film version of the novel: Liliana had had the very same intensity, the very same intensest charm. Looking back, she was to me a symbol of the potentiality for peace and for very great beauty in our human living, I might even say bearing the promise of our higher innocence in the future. Tolstoy had seen this spirit — which bore within itself a pure potentiality for our future humanity — in his own Russian folk, in Natasha. This spirit he associates with the idea of peace. In his own Russia, this great spirit had survived the Napoleonic wars matured and now ready for a still fuller future. I think of the image of Natasha at the end of the story sitting in the house of her fiancé Prince Andréi with his family after his death, quietly welcoming, in her newly ripened maturity, the adventurous Pierre who himself survives Andréi, as his closest friend. Natasha would make it through, but Liliana did not, and I would remain with her for another full year while she was in this general state of dismay and depression. But, insisting with me as she did more and more on a strict attachment to her family circle, which would have bound me to a very narrow life, I could not abide in the relationship, and so, we broke up.

After that time, I would only see her again once, when she called me to return a book of hers that I had kept. To this day I cannot say if Liliana had arranged for this meeting with the purpose of encouraging another start for us, but at our encounter at her family's house, the matter was never brought up through all the hospitality. There was a noble kindness towards me from both herself and her mother, as I remember them at the door bidding me good-bye for what would be the last time. After that last visit, I would not see Liliana again, though I continued to hear faint news about her married life and her children, from Christine and Luigi with whom I would continue to be linked for a long time to come. Of one thing I remained certain — that Liliana would undoubtedly have been over all this time a very worthy mother of her children, on whom no doubt she would have lavished a very great tenderness and care and a devotion that would know no bounds.

*

The last year I spent at university on my own would be a bleak one. I continued dissatisfied with the social life that was being offered to me by my peers, which seemed to me so abstract and chatty, conforming with the usual academic dryness, which no one could escape. I also remained, in spite of being the top student of my class, fundamentally alienated from virtually all the English teachers whom I had known, who seemed to me unable to assume any personal relationship or understanding with me. I continued to perform well at school but was otherwise dissociated from that setting in my deepest nature, which had in the meantime simply gone to sleep. Towards the middle of my last school year, I had even contracted chicken pox, which I had never had as a child.

Out of this dark time, however, came a hopeful return. I had developed, over the course of the year before then, a significant association with at least one of our teachers, through the mediation of the English student with whom I shared some pride of place while at university on account of our standing. Thomas Gary, whom I had befriended from the time of our participation in the "Tragedy" course, in his thinking and his writing both, was a mature intellect — it seemed to the rest of us, already well beyond our years, and indeed something of a prodigy. One incoming teacher, there for a short time, had likened his writing ability to that of Samuel Johnson. In our second-to-last year together at Loyola of Montreal, Gary had grown close to Joanne, an older woman of forty from Oxford University who taught in the department and was herself a sensation. I found myself, along with Gary, taking another course on Shakespeare with her, and it was over that time that Joanne conceived the idea of our carrying on our studies in England. I had in the meantime applied and won a Commonwealth Scholarship, which gave me the opportunity to study in England. I was to go to Norwich to study at the University of East Anglia. Gary, by now a couple with the separated Joanne, would go to Oxford to study, while she assumed teaching duties there. It was in my final month at Loyola that I also met the young woman who, nine months later while in England, would become my wife.

IV

I flew to England in late September of 1974, to be received in London by the British Council representatives who administered the Commonwealth Scholarship there. I stayed in residence for a few days at The University of London while attending the Orientation session the Council provided, before finally setting off for Norwich by train. Being in England was like returning to a childhood world where everything seemed once again small and quaint. The houses seemed all piled up one on top of the other, while the reverse traffic, which makes such an impression when one encounters it for the first time, had the effect of a reflexive existence, as if everything were being seen in a mirror. One had to take very special pains, when crossing the street, not to look the wrong way, and I finally settled the problem by looking in both directions wherever I undertook to cross.

It was the proverbially wet England. I remember it raining all the time. The Council had provided for my stay at a small hotel when I got to Norwich, to see me over to the following day when I might settle into residence at the University. It was exactly the England one always hears about. And so, distinctly I remember sitting down that evening to dinner at the hotel, when a very old woman, who was well into her late eighties, came up to me within a very few moments, and, bending over herself, suddenly shrieked out: "Cup a' tea!"

*

My course of studies in England, which led to a research degree, I had to direct myself, so that from that day onwards I became entirely self-educated. This was with the exception of the few consultations I would have with my supervisor, who was John Broadbent (a pupil of E.M.W. Tillyard). Beginning with the classical criticism of Horace, Longinus and Aristotle, and running through Sidney, I had very quickly arrived at Coleridge, who himself claimed my attention for some time. From there I went on to Dowden, then to Bradley, from which point I would undertake a thorough study of most of the major English criticism on Shakespeare up to my own time. I also went out of my way to read I. A. Richards and T. S. Eliot as well as William Empson. Broadbent had found my older historical approach to criticism unusual but also refreshing, and he thoroughly encouraged me to continue along that line, feeling that my work could only gain in depth. He had also dropped the hint that I might review the Renaissance philosophy, and so I had immersed myself in some of the classic work of Mirandola, Ficino and Vires. Broadbent was somewhat stunned that I had decided to read the philosophy at first hand, though this was not in the original. Kristeller and Cassirer had become my guides to the philosophy. To this I would add, in my second year, a study of the history of thought since the Renaissance, with Basil Willey as my guide, as well as a reading of the major classical epics, including Dante. I had also re-read all the major British poets with the intention of more carefully defining the characteristic thought and idiom in each case.

Arming myself continuously in this way, I had from the first year of work, of course, also plunged into Shakespeare himself. I read through the whole corpus consecutively, strenuously recording my perceptions in the margins of my Arden editions, while adding to my reading of Shakespeare the reading of his most influential first contemporaries: Marlowe and Kyd, principally. I had worked everything out to fill out the fullest possible background within the limited time I had. I read continuously for almost twelve hours a day, without strain, for the experience had entirely claimed me. On the other hand, I did have the habit of getting up rather late, largely because of the bad habit I had developed of reading intensely right up to bedtime, which always made the first few hours of sleep difficult.

I had made my topic of study on Shakespeare what had struck me as the governing ideal of his expression: passion as literal representation. The topic had immersed me in the literal value of Shakespeare's own word, where he seemed to be attempting to resolve the problematic duality between inner and outer reality.

That I had decided was the key to Shakespeare's (as well as the Elizabethan) intensity. His own intense effort of representation had thereby become my mental experience, a situation that could not bode well for me when I came to a play like *Macbeth*. For many nights, I had taken Shakespeare's struggle in *Macbeth* into my sleep, continuing to work out with him the problem of contending with evil even into my sleep consciousness.

The language of Shakespeare's plays had in this way become the very breath I breathed, the very consciousness I possessed. Study of this kind could only take place in conditions of extreme isolation, and that had indeed become my mode of life. Within two months of my arrival in England, I had moved out of residence into a house of my own, thanks to the very generous stipend I received from the Scholarship. By then I had been joined by Ivana who, in December of that year, would become my wife. It was she who had made arrangements for the renting of the house, which was tucked away down some picturesque lane in a remote suburb of Norwich. We had given little thought to how far we were from the University grounds — in fact, at the extreme opposite pole cartographically — so far, in fact, that in time I would only make the visit down to the University library once a week to gather all the books I needed for the week's reading. We remained consequently in our own little world, at some remove from the university's social setting, and had in effect become virtual recluses, except for the occasional visits to market in the City Center.

Ivana had also been an English student while at Loyola. Her family was from the region of Venezia, and she herself was born there. She had come to Canada with her mother when she was three, the father arriving a year later. Her father being from a Northern Italian family, she had inherited the pearly blue eyes of that region, though her hair was dark-brown, after her mother. For some reason she had been given the Russian name. Born into a strong Italian tradition, she was the epitome of wifely care and devotion, adding to this an indescribable gracefulness. One professor whom I had befriended while at Loyola, from my days at college, met with her briefly after I had gone ahead to England (she was picking up materials I had left behind), and he had described her to me in a letter as a "creature of light." We were married in an Anglican ceremony at a country church just beyond the suburb in which we lived.

We had chosen to walk the three miles of dirt road that led to the church, in the company of our one personal witness — a Palestinian economics student who had become my close friend from the first few weeks of my stay in residence. Ahmad was a well-built, short, bushy-haired young man, of quiet, sensitive ways who loved to recline and chat in his brotherly Arab way, usually over honey and almonds which he always seemed to have on his person. Intellectually gifted, he had made a life of socializing in the streets of Bhagdad while studying at University there, when all the other students had desperately to struggle to master their subjects and keep up with their work. In the last month before exams, he would settle down to study continuously, without break of any kind, and would invariably come first, to the great wonder of all his peers for whom he had become something of a prodigy. Our marriage ceremony was scheduled for five o'clock that afternoon, so by the time we set out it had already turned dark; we had not counted on such a long way and, so, arrived over half an hour late. We had made it just in time, for the ceremony would need to be gotten through by six, as no ceremonies can be held after that time.

I remember to this day the moment when we all three turned up from the dirt road into the churchyard that was marked with so many gravesites, as is the custom there. The Minister, who had patiently waited for us, stood in the open doorway of the church, his white robes fluttering in the draught, while the light of the church streamed through from behind him into the dark outside. He was a rather Romantic figure for a Minister, nothing like our notion of what a Catholic priest was, young and quite handsome, with a small family, and a great reader of literature as it turned out. Our only other witness for the event was an old church sexton, very poorly dressed, who discreetly held aloof from our party at the back of the small church, while the ceremony was in progress. I do not believe that we took a picture of him, though in my memory he continues to stand there forever. Within minutes, we were married before God, and the Minister seemed to us unusually approving of the quiet and earnest nature of the event. Afterwards, we walked the dark road back for three miles, refusing a ride, and celebrated at home with Ahmad over cakes and tea, taking a few more photographs.

*

In the spring of the following year, we took the occasion of my spring break to visit the Lake District of Romantic fame. Our sojourn took place a little too early in the spring, so that the natural surroundings seemed quite austere. That time of year was also too cold and damp for long trekking, but there was still enough in the singular impressive roll of those famous low-lying mountains to evoke the glory and the freshness of that great dream. These had been the mountains that Coleridge also loved to roam, and I could go back to this vivid memory without trouble when I sat down some years later to read about his own great experiences there in the latest biography on him. Grasmere would remain, in the extreme north of England, the northernmost point I have ever visited. We stood in the very house that Wordsworth made famous, in the very room where he had composed in the intervals between his long perambulations. I was astonished to think that so huge a man could abide to work in such cramped quarters, and that in such a very homely place great, expansive imaginations would find their sublime expression.

By the time summer had come around, I had been admitted directly into the Ph.D programme on the basis of the scope of the project I had conceived and the recommendations of the several professors at the University who had interviewed me about it. Ivana and I decided to celebrate with a trip to her home district in Italy, where we stayed for two months. We went over by ferry, and then by train via Paris, where we stopped for a few days. Finally, we arrived in Conegliano — Ivana's home town. I especially remember about our time there the indescribable magic of those warm Italian evenings when the air had freshened after a sultry day, when we would make our long way up the circular path to the top of the fortress hill around which the town was built, to take in, from the tratorria terrace where we dined, that misty view of the foothills of the Alps just beyond. We would make our way into those Alps later, staying for an entire month in a small village called Borzoi. The further view we had, while there, of the great interlocking valleys below, looking out from the vantage point of our high apartment perch, was of truly da Vincian majesty. Compared to the equally splendid Rockies, these mountains had the further addition of having been made habitable, with treacherous, serpentine roads that had made even the most distant points accessible, as is generally the case in Europe. Venezia is truly wonderfully situated, with these great mountainous areas of Treviso on the one side, and the balmy Adriatic seacoast, on the other: in each case, only a few hours away. Venice itself was but an hour's train ride from Conegliano. I would take primarily a geographic and aesthetic interest in this extraordinary city of islands.

Appropriately enough, it was not until we travelled down to Florence that I awakened to the great art that Italy offers. While in Paris briefly, I had stood before da Vinci's "Mona Lisa," and now in Florence it was "The Annunciation," also by da Vinci, that had captured my imagination. I had also been struck by the Donatello "David" which, remarkably, stands outside to this day, in the same square where Savonarola was burned. I had found most engrossing of all, however, those extraordinary scenes from the Testaments cut out in miniature sculpture by Ghiberti on the doors of the city's famous Baptistry: the "Doors of Paradise" as they are called. Of these Michelangelo no less would say that they deserved to be The Doors of Paradise. Ghiberti became for a while a very great passion of mine (though very strangely as I am writing this, I could not for a good half-day remember Ghiberti's name, the only one whose name I could not remember of those I mention here).

I would go out of my way on my return to Norwich to provide myself with a number of books that reproduced Ghiberti's sculptures. His depiction of the raising of Lazarus, especially when this sculpture is seen from up close — which I had the chance to do only with the books, had made the greatest impression on me of any art work I had seen until then. I had also been greatly astonished to discover Donatello's own "Annunciation" hidden away in a very dark corner of one of Florence's countless churches, and I would submit Donatello's work also to close scrutiny when I got back to England. No doubt there was some significance attached to the fact that my first exposure to art had taken the form of an encounter with the sculpture of the early Italian Renaissance. I was too immature in the appreciation of art at that time to be fully able to fathom, when in Florence, what it meant for me to stand also before Michelangelo's late "Pietà," known also as "The Deposition." In this work, Michelangelo sculpted himself as the figure of Joseph of Arimathea who supports the dead body of Jesus, and the head of Jesus and that of Mary, his mother (the one leaning against the other), are given to us in an especially poignant relation of completely shared love. So powerful is the impression this sculpture can make on one, I have no difficulty whatever going back to it in imagination today, and I can still see it there before me in *its* quite over-illuminated niche.

*

Just before we set out for Italy, we had moved quarters from 16 Kinsale Avenue to 61 Gowing Road, still in the same outlying parts of Norwich, though farther north. Ivana and I had (in our young and impressionable compassion) made the catastrophic mistake of allowing the former owner of the Kinsale house back in as a tenant. All freedom that we formerly had was lost, and we had to contend with the woman's quick re-assumption of her own place, to the point of submitting to her tyrannical dictations about her right to do as she pleased in her own home. By admitting her back into the house, we had bound ourselves legally and could do nothing to evict her. Nevertheless, our new quarters provided roughly the same quiet setting, though I remember far many more sounds of birds there, and the constant, usually nightly rumblings of airplanes readying for take-off or just landing in the distance, for we were in the remote vicinity of the town's airport. It was at this house that I began my first serious writing on Shakespeare: the piece that was to find print twenty-one years later as the second chapter of my second book, *Othello's Sacrifice*. It was immediately met with great approval by my new supervisor at East Anglia, Nicholas Brooke, a former student of A.P. Rossiter.

Encountering Nicholas, who was at this time one of the world's most reputable Shakespeareans, suddenly confirmed in actual experience the sense of Shakespearean tradition I had been so intensely cultivating in myself over the course of the entire year that preceded this encounter. Building in a purely inspirational way on this (at the time) very privileged association, I found myself suddenly achieving far more mature prose than I had thought myself capable of writing. I was determined to illustrate Shakespeare's ideal of a literal representation of passion through his deployment of three major conventions, one of which was the use of silence, and all that this direction imported of a final reliance on the actor's own extreme effort to represent passion on stage. I had written on one of these conventions (the piece that was to appear in my book) and would, as a matter of course, have normally continued with the next. But, for some reason, I was diverted to the first of the six tragedies I had also projected for further analysis of Shakespeare's ideal, beyond my treatment of the three conventions. Six plays had seemed to Nicholas too many: *Richard II* was the first of these plays, and *it* was to be, in any case, the fatal iceberg on which my mightily rigged academic ship would founder, all too suddenly and tragically. I was at a loss to say what the structural unity of Shakespeare's representation in the latter part of the play came to, or rather I had come to the understanding that what there was of unity was inchoate, and so, for the first time since I had begun to excel as a student, I was forced to admit my inability to express the case. I felt I had fallen into a black hole. I had over this time been preparing some of the critical background to the work I was projecting on *Hamlet*, but no writing on that work would emerge.

I decided to interrupt the work I had been doing on *Richard II* in order to take a short trip — for the first time, since I was married, on my own — down to Oxford to meet with Thomas Gary. Gary and Joanne had not been able to accommodate themselves to their new life together, and Gary was living on his own in residence. He had been unable to adapt to all of Joanne's four children, and he had come to the guilty (for him) realization that he did not love Joanne. He had himself fallen into a deep melancholy, which had the effect of a profound depression, and without knowing it at the time, I found myself sympathetically falling into the same depression. It was as if all the idealism that had propelled me in my studies up to this point had suddenly vanished, and I was to leave Oxford actually greatly resenting Gary's reception of me. When I returned to Norwich, I would be unable to continue with my work altogether and, within a few months, had applied for a leave from my Scholarship.

I remember sitting down with Nicholas at one of the local pubs and discussing the nihilism that had suddenly overwhelmed me. He tried to dissuade me from leaving, with the argument that I would not be able to find the time to continue my work while I had to make a living, adding that everyone lived with some form of nihilism in themselves to contend with. But his intervention was to no avail. I would return to Montreal in July of 1976 and, within a few months of being back, would learn of Gary's own return from Oxford and of Joanne's horrid suicide.

*

Gary had returned to Montreal to take up a teaching job as a language instructor at our alma mater, on the recommendation of another of his former professors there. He had by then successfully completed his Oxford B.A. It was from some stray encounter with someone connected with Loyola that I learned of Gary's return and Joanne's suicide. She had deliberately drunk herself to death, choking on her own vomit. And so had ended gruesomely the life of the one to whom I owed my going to England at all. Joanne had in the meantime given birth to their child — a girl, who now lived with Gary and his professor friend, Harry. Needless to say, Gary was tacitly held responsible for Joanne's death by all who had worked with her in the English department at Loyola, but no one who did not know Gary could realize just how sensitive or passive he had always been in his trials of love, or how remarkably acute he was in his understanding of them, and he would no doubt have taken the death, and his subsequent ostracization at work, very much to heart. But, as it turned out, I would never see Gary again, though I would regularly get news about a life that would continue to add tumult to tumult, until one day he would simply turn his back on it all and leave, to take up a reclusive residence in another city in the basement of his parents' apartment, while his parents undertook to help him care for his child. This is he who had been the most talented of our class and had held out the greatest promise.

*

Within a few months of my own return to Montreal, I had
landed a part-time job as a high-school teacher of English,
taking over from an older woman who for a time would
become my close friend and Ivana's. It was a general habit I
had of making, or always expecting to make, a personal experience out of every significant meeting that destiny had put in
my way. For this reason I did not take well to the kind of
strictly casual, non-commital approach that was taken to
meetings seemingly everywhere in the academic world. I had
been offered the teaching job by the former vice-principal of
the high school from which I had matriculated, who had in
the interim become principal of the school at which I would
work. The job had allowed us to move out from the home of
Ivana's parents to a third-storey flat on Papineau Street where
Masson crosses it. Our move had brought me into the vicinity
of the person who was to play a major role in my life, both
then and in later years.

I had met Antonio D'Alfonso through Luigi when they
had studied together in the film department at Loyola, just
before I left for England. Antonio, I learned, was now living
but a few blocks away. With him I would share, over the
course of the next two years, perhaps the most intense and
fruitful intellectual relationship I have had. Especially we
came to share a great passion for classical music. It was over
this time that I would listen with great intentness to the music
of Bach and Beethoven, principally the orchestral and sym-
phonic works. It was the grandest of releases from a hitherto
rigorously analytical intellectual life. Since my first exposure
to Beethoven and Stravinski, I had taken an intense interest,
for a brief time just before leaving for England, oddly enough
only in the 7th symphony and Mass of Anton Bruckner. How
those early experiences of music had gone into molding me

would be difficult to say, but from my new listening I would develop very suddenly a new sensitivity especially for the power of creative shaping, also a new appreciation for the inspirative faculty, that would entirely alter the approach I would make to my critical writing on Shakespeare in its next phase. What especially helped my maturation along as a critic who had to shape words was the intensive interest I had taken over this time also in the late quartet music of Beethoven and the many quartets of Mozart's middle and late periods, as well as the Cello suites of Bach — all of which I shared with Antonio.

Another major passion Antonio and I shared at this time was the poetry of T.S. Eliot. I have never since personally known a better reader of poetry than Antonio, who had trained intensively in structuralism. I remember distinctly to this day a conversation we had once about the evolution of Eliot's poetry from his early to his middle period. Antonio had been grappling with what became of Eliot's obsession with waste beyond the first main stage of his work. We determined that the experience of waste had transmuted itself into the idea of profiting spiritually from forgetfulness. The ease with which such discoveries passed between us, as though it might be one experience to us both, was one of the rarest and most significant intellectual experiences I have had. I had, along such a route, turned my attention consequently more fully to Eliot whom I was quite determined to write about. I had prepared for this by applying for a Canada Council Fellowship that would allow me to go to the University of Toronto where, as part of an M.A. programme, it was my plan to write a thesis on Eliot, Dylan Thomas and Ted Hughes (the work of which latter two I had also submitted to intense study over this period). I would in this way, I thought, be able to make the fullest use of my time while away from my Shakespeare thesis. I was awarded the Fellowship, after an interview, on the basis of a thesis proposal that I had submitted under the title "The Sudden Illumination" (a phrase from T.S. Eliot). The thesis was to be a study of the tradition of the ecstatic "moment" in modern poetry and what this might be taken to signify as an idea of redemption for our time. I was to concentrate on the "Four Quartets" (by Eliot), "In Country Sleep" (by Thomas) and "Gog" (by Hughes). All this had been scheduled for the fall of 1977.

My stint as an English teacher in high school had, in the meantime, brought me a following of some of my best students, one of whom, after her graduation, would introduce me to her family. They spoke to me about a cottage they had by the seaside in Nova Scotia, to which they had not been for some years, and this they made available to me. I could take some time to get away and carry on some of the writing I felt in need of doing, after nearly a year of teaching duties that had left me with no time for such work at all. I ended up in one of the most unpromising places I have ever been to, which, with complete aptness, I might call "the world's end." It is the only place of the kind I have ever known. Larry's River was the name of the village, though it was more of a spot than a village. Most, if not all of the men in that place were unemployed, and I very soon learned, from some of my friend's relatives who actually lived there, that for the most part these men would get into violent, drunken scuffles whenever they could. At my first approach to the village on foot, I had been immediately spotted and was to be addressed by a young woman who would ask me about my stay. I told her where I was headed and did she know where they lived? When I got to the relatives, I found out from them, among other things, that this was the village whore, who also happened to be married.

I had gone over to the house where I was to stay to find that the floors were very moldy from the dampness of the several years over which the house had been neglected. It had also been damp in the recent period before my arrival, and I can only remember, with the exception of a brief time, a general and unrelieved sombreness from the continual clouds that seemed to overhang the cove as if stuck there. I decided to air out, on my first day, most of the items that would prove necessary for my stay and period of work, including the mattress to at least one of the beds. I had just placed this item over the railing of the front balcony when suddenly to my side from the back of the house, there sprung up from the tall grass the same young woman who had accosted me at the village limits. She approached me, warming slightly, and re-marked with some affectation of sociability: "Well, there'll be one more light in town tonight."

With some discomfort, I managed to extricate myself from her company for the time being, but, when it had turned dark, and late into the night, I began to dread the thought that, ignored by me, perhaps this woman would pretend with her husband that I had made some attempt on her. Perhaps he would come to this dark corner of the village (for the house was set apart at the extreme end to the village) and retaliate on me. Oppressed with these thoughts, I went to bed with a couple of carving knives that I had taken for protection. I managed to fall asleep but was, very shortly, violently awak-ened by a horridly frightening sound, which turned out to be the knives themselves, which had fallen to the floor from their resting places under the mattress. I was determined not to sleep in the house another night, and I was to spend the remaining few days, of what would become a short stay, over at the relatives, on the pretext that the other house was too damp to sleep in.

Before I left the village, however, I was to have another remarkable experience. I had set out for a certain section of the sea-coast that had a beach, and I had made my way there by truck after being picked up along the road. From this moment began the experience that I was to subsequently work up into the only short story I have ever written. More of a prose poem, I called it "Marina," after the girl of nineteen who bore that name, who was among the others in the truck that had picked me up. All this seemed very extraordinary to me, considering that I was, at this very time, projecting work on Eliot, who had written his own poem called "Marina." My prose poem records my experience of Marina's own situation quite literally (including the very conversations that were exchanged at the time), with some allusion to Eliot's poem, as I thought fit. My Marina was a sensitively intelligent and very quiet university student, though she had the friendliest and most confident attitude of the group of girls I had met who kept company with me on the beach.

I was later to take the long walk with Marina alone around the cape that led back from the beach to the village, and we would stop to sit together on a large rock that stood right up against the water. It was the only time during my stay that I remember the sun shining through, in the way my prose poem speaks of. She lay with her back against me, as we sat on the rock huddled into each other. I could not have thought of any other kind of relationship with Marina beyond some (perhaps not so) simple caressing of her head, and I did not even kiss her, though I did not hide any of my great admiration of her in that moment. I was just young enough still, and looked still younger, so that she might well have expected anything from me, and she seemed to actually grow disenchanted when nothing very serious happened. We made arrangements to meet again that evening at a wharf by the water in the village, but she never showed up, sending her friends to meet me instead — it seemed to me as if they all thought I might be taking an interest in one of them. They all knew about the afternoon I had had with Marina, for we talked about her freely. In the meantime, Marina had left her address with me; I left "the world's end" the next morning and, returning home, wrote the poem that I sent her, with fresh thoughts in a letter saying how beautiful she had appeared to me during our time together. But she never wrote back, and I am wondering in this present moment, for the first time since that experience, what my prose poem — the only work of its kind I have written — may have meant to her over all these intervening years.

Marina

Of the party of young girls whom he had joined along the beach, she alone had shown any depth of character. In the open ride by truck into the bay, among the others, brown hair blown over the mouth, she had exuded an intrinsic beauty that seemed to him uncommon for her age. It was not a beauty anyone could see, least of all the local boy who had recently dropped her from lack of interest, eager for rougher game. To others, it might not appear to be any special beauty. She was short and she had a small body, though she was fair and her body was soft and tight. Yet he knew better than to make light of a budding daughter in whose sight the country air was bathed in softness. She was without the hardness one associated with the country, without the hardness one expected of adolescence above the trembling insecurity underneath. Behind the mild embarrassment that came from addressing him as an older, male stranger, he detected a young woman eager for recognition such as the country would never provide. And he wondered whether under the clutch of its influences, she would ever be permitted to fulfil her dreams. Then, under a shaft of sunlight, her forehead bared to the wind, beneath a sudden gust of lilac and the faint bittersweet smell of sea carried from the bay, she spoke her name, and he knew her as Marina.

Later, as she lay stretched out along the beach among the others, she was lost to the group's gossip about a local girl who had recently fallen to violence. He suddenly felt withdrawn and isolated. Perhaps she was half-aware of him as he lay stretched out beside her propped up at an angle. He wondered how far she could see into the heart of beauty, how far she could be encouraged to feel and not be afraid. He wondered if she too could see the rock mounds bulging out through the mist at sea, heat-cracked and earth-brown, as he saw them. When he asked her if she would join him for a walk around the cape, in a tone that expressed some surprise and a sensitive excitement, she said she wouldn't mind.

Later on, as they walked along the sea alone, his arm around her, he admired her for her soft yielding warmth and her quiet confidence. It was something he might have expected, he felt he ought to have expected it of her. Yet as they walked he was aware of a mild dread in her of the unexpected, even though he liked to think that, under the caressing weight of his hand over her head, she felt he offered her a depth of warmth and a protectiveness different in its lack of threat. He thought of those who could not bend, who could not bow the spirit to be reborn. He thought deeply of hardness. He thought of how much of that there was in her and in him. As they walked, he was aware of the cape slipping behind them and of the sandline along the west shore, which they had trod, exposed to view as they veered into the cove. As they approached a large, flat rock washed smooth by the motion of ages, and brilliant under the beat of sun, he looked down at her, and she stared back up through eyes that he had seen in dreams. Above the amethyst glare of jellyfish and the dark, vermilion spread of sea-weed under feet, she stared out in innocent dread from a world that had crowned her long before the hard, swift gripe and muddy burying of sceptres.

Later still, propped up against the rock, she leaned her back lightly against his breast, and he locked his arm across the top of her breast, shoulder to shoulder. In response to his prodding banter, she stared up confessing to a half-formed attraction to him out of the dark of the dance-hall the night before, though he had not really recognized her there, and it was only now that he recognized the same eyes he remembered glancing up at him when, for a moment in the dark, they had stood at each other's side. After surveying the spread of cape and sea, lost to the haze of horizon, he buried his face in her hair, under the crown of her head, breathing the sharp sweet smell of sunlight and saltsoft heat. While he paused to stare into the wash of water lapping the shoreline rocks, she continued to lie in a quiet expectancy.

Out in the bay a wild duck, dark-brown, brown out of bayline wood, dark-edged, stooped suddenly out of sight behind the glare of water. She would never know her real beauty, he told himself. After the stubborn denials that had left her neglected and alone, in the whirl of influences that would rush her into attitudes more easily borne, he wondered if she would ever be permitted a glimpse into the heart of light, if she would ever gain sight of the beauty one could not speak of, one could not point to — bone beauty — beyond grasp of man or strength of woman to shoulder. O my daughter!

Once again, he was aware of the tension he had felt when they had first set out below the rising sound of surf, from the difference between them in age and experience, and the silence deepened between them. As the fog seeped slowly into the cove, settling imperceptibly over the near-distant villages, a foghorn began to blow with a dim moaning, resounding from all sides, and he asked her where it came from. Suddenly, before he knew what he had set loose, he caught himself asking her many questions, filling up the silence quickly, formulating many questions, about the bay, about the wood and the foghorn, about her shyness and her beauty . . . behind the water, out of sight, shrieking words! the rush of sea-voices in the wind! In a tone which masked some perplexity and a new irritation, but always that quiet expectancy, that bated dread, she remarked that he asked too many questions.

All this while, she lay quietly against him and he against her, and her crown of head, beneath his hands, burned in the longlost sun . . .

As she lay back against him, hunched into herself, arms on knees, it seemed to him that she expected everything and asked for nothing. Yet under a strange caress whose lingering tensions she did not expect, which she could not understand, her expectancy deepened into irritation, her irritation into hardness, and she was aware through her pleasure of the cold sea-winds that came with the seep of fog. Soon, as the weight of the wind grew heavier and colder, she unfurled the lumpish bundle she had been carrying with her, and after glancing back at him quickly, she spread her frock out — spreading brilliance! bonewhite on rockash! Then, after shifting to fasten and fix the frock, she settled back, peering up at him with that strange intensity, again with that look of dread, more insecure now, deeper and harder. But though he lay close to her and clung to her more tightly, though the weight of her back grew stronger against him, though they huddled, they could not contain the cold freshness of the wind that made her shiver in the deep sunlight. And very soon she was cold.

Late that evening, under a barren field below the village, he sat ruminating alone, a dark heap on a rock-pile pier, struggling against the cold clasp of damp . . .

Though there could be no end to his caressing, no end to the beauty that lingered round sea-voices deeper than the sea, for the first time he was aware of the hardness in her as they prepared to leave, and he began to feel a deep uneasiness. The way back round the basin to the village would be rougher now, the woodland thicker and more ominous, the isolation deeper, and cold round rocks hard under the feet! Before he stood to go, he paused for a

moment to ponder the light of the bay suddenly grown
harsh and distant, and he thought of her standing above
him — himself on the sand! herself on the rock! — and of
her deepening disappointment, hardness provoking hardness! He told himself that he would see the dying light right
through into the dark, and right through into the cold. But
it was then that he looked up and caught sight of her still
staring down at him, and his mind buckled under the
weight of the dread suddenly pulling them together. In
bonewhite frock that answered to the brilliance of the sun,
under brownfired glare of eyes of mouth that caressed even
as they cursed, even as they lifted, she burned above him!
O daughter of the sea!

*

In the fall I would go to the University of Toronto to com-
mence work on my Masters project, but that would not last
long. I had appropriately registered into a course on Shakespearean Tragedy, but with a professor whose condescending
banality I saw as a frighteningly backward prospect for myself
personally. I had also registered into a course on Modern
Poetry which focused on Hardy, Lawrence and Edward
Thomas — the only course offered in the general area of Eliot.
I had altered my thesis proposal in the meantime, almost one
year after I had been awarded the Fellowship, to accommodate the advance I had made with my study of Eliot. I now
planned a work entirely on Eliot — from his early work
through his later — with reference to the principles of associa-
tionism that I saw as central to his work. I had thought of
placing Eliot in this way within a tradition that would yoke
him with Wordsworth who had built explicitly on these principles in his famous "Preface." That had struck me as a bold
suggestion worthy of argument since, of course, Eliot had, in
part, established himself by taking exception to Wordsworth's

theories of poetry, in the equally famous essay "Tradition and the Individual Talent." To argue that Eliot retained a secret understanding of Wordsworth's theories, which he might have kept secret even from himself and on which he built in his poetry — that argument would certainly have caught the attention of the academic world for which I wrote. To this day I continue to believe that the main great line of criticism in English tradition remains, from the mid-eighteenth century onwards (see Jackson Bates, *From Classic to Romantic*), through Wordsworth and Coleridge right up to Eliot himself, the line that theorizes the Imagination as primarily an *associative* faculty. The Imagination brings a number of *living* thoughts together in such a way that they *pass over into* one another, as "the human spirit effects the joining of thought-masses *only in accordance with* their content" (so, Rudolf Steiner).

The course on Modern Poetry was given by Michael Kirkham, who strangely enough had gotten the job through an interview with Nicholas Brooke. At the time Clifford Leech had been the chairperson at the University of Toronto, and since Kirkham had applied for the job from England and Nicholas had formerly worked for Leech at Durham, Nicholas had been asked to conduct the interview from over there (an unorthodox procedure by today's standards). The effect of Nicholas's re-appearance in my life was the opposite of what one might expect. Rather than re-inforcing my sense of my position at the University of Toronto, it harkened me back to my doctoral thesis, which would have remained untouched over the course of the year. That thought hit hard at the time, while the work I was doing in my courses seemed to me tediously slow and far afield from my own active imagination. The idea that in fact Hardy, Thomas and Lawrence were the major poets of the early century and the main sources of later poetry in the century struck me as perverse and in any case not to my purposes. The consequence was that after two months at Toronto, I gave up the Fellowship and returned to Montreal to continue work on my thesis on Shakespeare.

The sense of creative ordering that I had quietly been acquiring from my intensive listening to music earlier that year, as I believe, suddenly bore fruit in what I thought some of the best writing I had done up to that point. It was in the late fall and early winter of that time that I produced the material that was, almost untouched, to form (some fourteen years later) the second and third chapters (on "Sexuality" and "Revenge") of my first book on Shakespeare — though, immersed in the structure of the thesis, I could hardly forsee that prospect at the time.

I had moved to Toronto on my own, Ivana staying behind at the apartment in Montreal — hence the possibility of my returning there. Over the intervening years since our marriage, obsession with my intellectual and creative work had continued to the neglect of my life with her, while at the same time her unfulfilled presence had become a major distraction from my continuing work, and in the next few months we would think of separating, Ivana taking her own apartment for a time. We could not leave each other, however, and by the time summer had arrived we had conceived the idea of time together again in Italy, where we would stop before I resumed my Scholarship in England for a final year. While in Conegliano, I completed yet another section of my thesis — the last of the material on *Hamlet,* which was to form, in this case entirely untouched, the last chapter of my first book (on "Death"). I had gone into the writing inspired by my appreciation of the prose writing of F.R. Leavis in his book *New Bearings in English Poetry.* His view that the seminal poets of the century were Hopkins, Eliot and Pound was in startling contrast with what I had been expected to accept while at Toronto. Apart from my work, however, very little else engaged me during my stay in Italy, except for one extraordinary incident that took place in a region just outside Vittorio Veneto. We had gone, with some of Ivana's cousins, to visit a grotto of some reputation, from which at a certain point three women walked out into view with an aura that suggested their emergence from an initiation site. A single olive tree stood by the entrance of the cave. It was an image that greatly struck my imagination at the time because of an account I had read by Eliot of a similar moment of extraordinary intensity in his own life when he had witnessed three men playing cards on the ground by a mill, a scene that served as the inspiration for a similar image that appears in his poem "The Journey of the Magi."

Come fall, I was on my way to England once again, this time alone, Ivana staying behind in Venezia. On arriving, I had made the acquaintance of a Turkish couple of great charm, while momentarily in residence. They were young, and fair, very good-looking, and they had just had a child. Ugurhan had come to East Anglia — as had Ahmad years before — to study Economics, and he and his wife Talya were to remain my close friends over the whole of that last year in England. Meeting them had set off the thought of a child and a family for myself and Ivana, and I had in the meantime telegraphed Ivana to say that her place was with me. Jasmin, my first child, would be born in England in June. Much of that year would be spent in the joy of anticipating that birth, while Ugurhan and Talya looked on as godparents of a sort.

In my first term back, I would successfully complete what would become, very largely, the first chapter (on "Sorrow") of my book-to-be, though this was tucked away at the time in the long Introductory Part of the thesis. I had managed to establish a serious routine of work, which I kept to, for as long as we lived outside the city limits, in the country at a place called the Retreat. We had rented a section of a country house from a lady who also lived there. I would be driven into town (for a sum) by a neighbour and returned in the evening, working the entire day at the University library. This had been quite unlike my former work routine, which had been conducted entirely out of my own space at home. Oddly enough, however, when we moved into the city just before Christmas, within a very short distance from the University, on Mill Hill Street, all work on my thesis ceased. I was only about twenty-five pages away from rounding out a view of the entire work but did not know it at the time. I simply could not see my way through. The rest of the winter would be spent doing some intensive reading of my own. It was then that I read in depth: Freud, Jung and Nietzsche, as well as the complete poetry of Dylan Thomas, W.H. Auden and Wallace Stevens, by way of extending my intellectual experience of the twentieth century.

V

By the end of July we had flown back to Montreal, where we would set up home for what seemed to us the first time. This was to be my first period of almost complete freedom from academic life. I had more or less renounced it, having concluded this time that I would never be returning to my thesis. I had found a job as a language teacher in a private school that would keep me at work every morning, but in the afternoon I would return home to the freshly found wonder of a new life which consisted of hardly anything other than continual dandling and adoring of Jasmin, for the most part in the luxurious lap of our great Victorian couch that we had just re-upholstered in vivid materials and over which Ivana had draped some hand-knit crochet work depicting a great peacock displaying itself. This was at one end of a long open room, as great music streamed continually towards us from the other end. I was not altogether idle in this period, however. I had in the meantime conceived the idea of publishing two local poets, with Luigi's financial backing; my purpose was to set forth the poets in the context of a critical introduction intended to bring out the full intricacies and subtleties of the poems in sequence, and so, in demonstration of what it meant to be "significant" as a poet — hence, the title of the projected series: "Significant Poets."

One of the poets I had fixed on — Orin Manitt — I had come across while teaching in high school some few years before; I remembered being struck at the time by the fine technical quality of the poems he had written. The other — Robert Penee — was an English graduate from Loyola, now languishing as a hard-working provider for his family (they also had one child). Penee had impressed me on my departure from Loyola some few years earlier, especially by the combination of his abstract remoteness (which only seemed accentuated by his great bearded face, so striking in one so young) and his unusually sensitive thoughtfulness and courtesy, beautifully concentrated on the other. When I visited him to talk over the project, he introduced me to the music of Schubert, which I had never listened to before. What stood out for me especially was the stunning later quintet with two cellos, which was to become a kind of signature piece for me in the next period of my life. My exposure to that music was to be a kind of overture to a whole new phase of life that would bring me in touch with Europe again in a way I could not have dreamed of. In the end, I was forced to choose between the two poets for economic reasons and settled on Manitt, because of the better reception he received from Harry, the Loyola professor, whom I thought an especially judicious reader, although Penee's work also struck me as both richly imaginative and profound. Looking back on this episode, however, I have to feel that I made the wrong choice, especially since nothing more came of the publishing venture, which stopped at Manitt. Publishing Penee would have allowed him to draw on the further support that the Canada Council of Arts bestowed on authors who had become published, and that would have meant some financial security for Penee and his family. Manitt on the other hand had been well set up as a high school teacher for years. Manitt's work probably engaged my critical faculties more intensely than Penee's, but the choice I made remains to me for all that the wrong one, which today I might wish to undo.

Manitt became in that time of my life, however, a symbol: in him was configured the whole of my most recent phase of life, in which my long critical-intellectual training had

momentarily come to a head in a study of Yeats, and as Manitt
seemed to me in his own vision Yeatsian (Manitt was himself
Irish), it appeared to me as if my reading had once again
momentarily mingled and merged with my life-experience,
modest as the concurrence was in this case.

*

Penee, on the other hand, was heralding in the next phase of
my life, hauntingly forecasted in the Schubert piece I had
learned about from him. I had over a short tenure established
something of a reputation at the language school and had
now become a teacher of the advanced group. Among these
were a number of Iranian students who had just escaped from
the political turmoil in Iran, for this was December, 1979.
There were also a few Europeans in the group: one Michel, a
middle-aged Frenchman from Paris, and Judit, a young Hungarian woman of twenty three, who was just out of university
in Debrecen. For a long time I was to remain altogether unaware of the romantic feelings Judit had been quietly nursing
about me — for she had a profoundly sensitive, almost purely
introspective nature. However, I was to learn later that over
the entire month of instruction they had had with me, Michel
had continually been kidding Judit about her "Beloved
Teacher," the phrase that unbeknownst to me had passed
regularly between them on paper as they sat in the group.

Not until the Christmas farewell party at the end of
term, which was (in keeping with the school schedule) held
in the morning, did I become quite consciously aware. I remember another new student of mine questioning me, as she
stepped into the teacher's lounge whence the party had origi-
nated, as to whether Judit was not my wife. Judit was at that
moment sitting quietly in the center of the room, with that
young womanly intellectual grandeur about her that made

her look so wifely. Playfully I had replied that she was, and the answer seemed not less perfectly natural to our questioner. Later that morning I ensured that Judit would be dancing with me at some point, and that dance was to become the *primum mobile* of our sudden absorption in each other. We arranged to meet again the following afternoon for an outing, about which I can remember only one significant incident on our way back to her cousin's home. We had gotten lost in a neighborhood with which I was not familiar, so that Judit had had to call home to let her relatives know where we were, and, while waiting, we found ourselves at a school gymnasium where a basketball match was in progress. I remember only my putting my hand up against the wall for support as we watched when Judit lay her own hand over mine. Nothing more came of the moment, for I continued to assume the restraint that I thought was imposed upon me by my being married (and Judit was aware of my marriage, for I had brought a picture of Ivana and Jasmin to school to show my class).

Later that night I was driven home by Judit's male cousin, Judit being with us, and I distinctly recall glibly referring to the apartment building where I lived as "my solitary tower" — which is indeed what my apartment was later to become, to my great distress. We met again the following day — a Saturday, during which I remember holding and admiring Judit's beautiful hands, but again nothing came of this — until it was time for me to put her on the subway train. Then the dykes were drawn back, and we were in that moment so passionate and so complete in our kissing of each other, as we lay up against the station platform wall, that a station attendant had had to come around to caution us against the impropriety (more a matter of the Montreal Transport Commission's repressive distaste for public displays of intense passion on its premises). We continued for another good half hour in a more discreet section of the station setting, until it had simply become time for us to say goodbye. I would put Judit on the subway train, and the next day she would be flying back to Hungary. Unless she elected to call me, there would be no possibility of my stopping her from leaving, since I had been left with no way of reaching her.

I was suddenly plunged into the despair of being cut off from someone with whom I had fallen deeply in love. I would write to her Hungary address immediately, while she herself would write me almost as soon as she arrived there. Both of us realized what a mistake it had been to separate, though the despair would only be heightened as the further realization set in that, if there was to be any hope, it was I who would have to visit her in Hungary (since a second trip so soon out of that communist country would not at that time be possible). We began an intense correspondence, over the course of which we planned my visit for the spring. I became acquainted through travel books with the very great romantic beauty of Hungary, and I even undertook to learn the language. Over this long wait, I would only grow more fondly in love with Judit, and she with me, but the cultural and political displacements, not to mention the fact that I had a family, could only make our love acutely painful to us from the start. (Ivana had, in the meantime, learned of the "affair" and was quietly and indulgently bearing with it.)

Steeped in this tragic separation, I concentrated myself on the Schubert piece that Penee had introduced to me, which seemed to touch on just the chords that now resounded in me. It was the piece that Judit and I would share over this long time of separation. I listened also to Beethoven's Rasumovsky Quartets, and to Haydn's Quartets Opus 34, which I also discovered in this period. The whole experience opened up to me a sphere of life that I had, to that time, never really considered. I had suddenly been plunged into an encounter with Central Europe that the Schubert piece especially high-lighted for me — as if I might actually be in Vienna with Judit, dancing to Schubert's waltz from that last great movement. I found myself also living into the inspiration of that piece's second movement, as I shared, with Schubert, the distress of acute longing to overcome in imagination the bounds of time and space that separated me from Judit. Parts of this piece, like the Beethoven Quartets to which I was also listening, would evoke strongly the flavor of a gypsy romanticism that I would find myself associating with Judit's Hungary. It was my way of knowing her and being with her while we were cut off.

It was over this long and painful winter that I was to write the critical exposition to Orin Manitt's poems. I would go into the language school to teach in the morning and return home to work at the introduction in the afternoon, devoting myself to this critical effort for almost five months, until I was quite certain that the text was right. *Adam 2000* became the title of the volume, after the poem by that title. It almost felt as if I was working at some poetic production myself. Judit had been its inspiration. However, when spring finally arrived, I had decided to put off the trip to Hungary.

Sadly, over the course of our correspondence over those months, an element of doubt and suspicion had entered into the tone of our writing, at first in a way that was only implied. I had felt in Judit's tone, almost from the very first, a certain irony and distance that I had found hard to reconcile with our actual professions of affection and faith. Needless to say, my perception of that distance in Judit from an early stage had contributed substantially to the distress with which I was wrestling. Here I was about to give up my family for a rela-tionship that was more than uncertain and as yet untried. When the matter of her distance was finally broached as a reason for my putting off my trip, Judit had responded by fully acknowledging her feelings once again, though she admitted to a distance she said she had assumed out of consideration for my situation with my family; about this, she said, she felt that I would have to decide for myself.

Things would only confound themselves further later when, in response to Judit's renewed profession of being in love, I proposed in turn a visit for the summer. However, she did not consider that a good idea, she said, because summer in Hungary was not nearly so splendid as the fall, insinuating at the same time that she now had a "friend" with whom she would be going away on a trip to the Soviet Union. What else was she to do, she pleaded, for *I* had someone, she said, whereas *she* did not, and was she to remain alone? With these revelations, things fell apart for me irreversibly, and there never would, in the end, be a trip to Hungary. I would spend the rest of that summer in a cloud of despair, hankering after a life into which I had been given a rare glimpse, though any actual experience of that life had finally been denied to me.

*

It had been more of a dream of a new romantic cultural life than any actual prospect of a real life. Nevertheless the dream itself had been strong enough to put me in a state of readiness that I could not deny when another East European woman, of Jewish descent, appeared at the school, who greatly absorbed me. She had recently arrived from Israel where she had lived since she was seven, though she was born in Romania of a Romanian mother and a Russian father. Her husband (a Moroccan Jew) had decided on the move to Montreal in order to join his own family there, and they had come over with their two young children, in spite of the fact that the decision had not sat well with this woman. She had been through much distress over emigrating. She had made quite an impression on me with her fair hair, and she had a romantic air about her of a warm foreign land. I had been struck especially with her powerful self-absorption and great inner imagination, which took the form in her of a rather peculiar kind of lethargic genius.

She appeared in the advanced class at the school towards the end of the summer, in late August. Earlier that summer I had had a habit of stopping, in the morning before class, to sit on a particular bench in a garden of pear trees at the back of Christ Church Cathedral. The entire garden would later be (disastrously) uprooted, to make room for a new architectural edifice and a general expansion of revenues for the Church that included its approval for the creation of a giant underground mall under the Church itself, which is known today as "Les Boutiques Cathédrales." One morning, I found Pnina sitting quite alone in that very same spot on that same bench that I had made my own, reading the Torah, in Hebrew. From that time onwards I would suspect a profound connection between us, of the terms of which, however, I had little actual inkling.

I would, soon after this time, invite Pnina home to meet Ivana and to see Jasmin. Pnina seemed on that occasion overwhelmingly in admiration of our household. Not long after, she would invite Ivana out to the city's main exhibition area on Île Ste. Helene, the Terres des Hommes, with Jasmin and a few other folk; I had remained behind in the apartment. A little time after the party would have arrived at their destination, Pnina called in to say that she needed to speak to me. Since she sounded desperate, I agreed to meet with her and recall our sitting on a bench under that great grove of trees on the south side of Mt. Royal where the mountain dips down towards the Avenue des pins. With little reserve and considerable despair, she proceeded to confess to being in love with me. She had never wanted to come over from Israel, she said

— she had put up much resistance to the whole idea (how far she would go in her resistance, I would learn only later). However, overwhelmed with the eventuality of her coming over, she had consulted with a fortune teller who had offered her the consolation that she would meet up with "a friend" in Canada. She knew for certain now that I was that "friend"; she had known this from the time I had first stepped into the classroom as her teacher, she said, though despairingly she could not know what to make of her feelings about me.

After that encounter, we would take a few more walks on the Mt. Royal, and I especially remember on the occasion of one of these walks a very peculiar eruption, as we followed the great circular dirt road that leads back down the mountain on the east side to the Avenue du parc. Suddenly, out of the tall grass that bounded the road, an elderly woman, very colorfully dressed, in red and green, sprang up in front of us, inveighing against us for having disturbed her, innumerable pigeons flying up from around her at that same moment from our interruption of their feeding. The incident struck me as extraordinary, corresponding exactly as it did, I realized, to Pnina's own psychological condition at this time. For, while I had been from the first compassionate and friendly towards her in her overtures, I had remained both sexually and romantically aloof, and no doubt this was frustrating her greatly. I could not help feeling overwhelmed in this moment by the imaginative power it seemed to me Pnina had demonstrated by invoking in the outer world an occurrence which was the exact expression of the frustration she had been experiencing inwardly. I was overtaken with admiration of this profound relationship to nature, while in the meantime all the feelings that I had been privately harboring towards her as an east European, who played directly into my romantic predisposition towards that culture, could no longer be contained.

Both Ivana and Pnina's husband would know of the affair from the start, the husband going so far as to meet with Ivana in private to discuss how it was that she could tolerate it. Yet she did tolerate it, as he did also. By October, Pnina had insisted with her husband, who was fairly well off, on an apartment for herself. Here she would be able to return to the abstract painting that her professors had praised her for while at university. I continued at my job as a language teacher in the morning, and generally the afternoons would be ours. However, I remained for all this substantially by Ivana's side, a frame of mind that could not sit well with Pnina, and I remember one early Sunday afternoon Ivana and I dining at our home when the phone rang: Pnina needed me with her, she said, and could I come on over to the apartment right away. I told her that I would, after I had had my dinner, and that I would call her after I had done. When I did call later, however, there was no answer, and my mind ran wild with fears, since I was by then well-informed about Pnina's past attempts at suicide.

Only recently she had made one such attempt, unhappy with the idea that she would have to move to Canada, and now that she had come over, I had become her only hope of survival, she had said. Her husband was a Moroccan businessman with whom she had run away to escape from her parents, and he offered her no possibility of genuine imaginative understanding or sympathy. I was the one who could offer her all that she lacked in this regard, all that she knew was essential to the very soul-life of both of us. I hastened over to the apartment, fearing the worst, and indeed there was no answer when I knocked at the apartment door, though the door gave way when I tried it. The apartment, which was almost entirely bare, was dispossessed of all furniture except for Pnina's paintings. When I finally reached the far end of it, I found Pnina lying on her side on her cot on the floor, her

eyes staring outwards in despair. She was, somewhat excit-
edly, conscious of my arrival. I asked her why she hadn't
picked up the phone; my distressed concern was obvious, but,
in spite of the attention I was giving her, our conversation
would only frustrate her the more, since I could only re-iterate
my primary commitment to Ivana and to our daughter Jasmin. Standing up from her cot, Pnina made her way to the
bathroom where I discovered her, many minutes later, with a
plastic bag over her head. She had not been in this position
long enough that I could not intervene in time to divert her
from her intention, but the incident would mark me to the
point of a complete change in my life.

I became from that time onwards more and more committed to Pnina. Perhaps it was from pride that I could ever
be afflicted with a suicide that I would have caused (for I was
convinced by Pnina's attempt); perhaps it was from the sort
of idealism that would not accept my being the cause of
frustrated love or of frustrated imagination, quite apart from
any prospect of suicide. However that may be, by January
Pnina had found work for herself, and she was renting an
apartment large enough to have her two children with her. I
had in the meantime given up my job at the language school
to devote time once again to my thesis. Very soon I was
staying overnight in a regular way with Pnina and the children; I would work on my thesis in the morning and, in the
afternoon, would make my way over to my apartment on de
Normanville where I would keep Jasmin. Ivana had in this
latest interval elected to look for a part-time job, and she had
found one.

Things continued thus until early spring when a decision about where I stood seemed forced upon me. I had found
the adjustment to life with Pnina's children somewhat difficult: it was strange to be so suddenly fathering someone else's
children. I had also found it more than awkwardly strange to

witness the children's father still running errands for the family and intrusively appearing at the door every evening. I did not feel I could carry on in such circumstances and despairingly conveyed my thoughts along these lines to Pnina: we would have to give up thinking of a life together, I had said — though Pnina met this resolve of mine with the strangest calm — while I went on to lament the loss the end of our relationship would mean in respect of our shared imagination: I was no less in despair, I said, because I could never hope to have that kind of relationship with Ivana.

I then remember a corresponding moment with Ivana at our de Normanville residence later. Even more strangely, I found myself unable to make the leap back to her. I found myself saying, in yet another and the worst state of despair thus far, that I was unable to resist the pull of fate Pnina was exercising over me. I told Ivana that I did not feel that I had the power any longer even to choose to return to her, that it seemed all predetermined for me. I remember languishing miserably in this thought and being entirely overcome. Beyond that fateful moment, which would change my life irreversibly, I can recall one further incident of poignant hopelessness — when I returned to claim my belongings from the de Normanville apartment. In a despair that I can barely face even now as I recall the moment, Ivana stood before me in what had been our former bedroom, and, without snatching at me, and entirely in that generous way of hers that could only ever leave me free in my person, she was appealing to me, as it were for one last time, in saying how very much alone she was feeling.

It was a force of sheer will that kept me going in my commitment to Pnina from that time, overwhelmed as I was by the great turmoil of feelings that were swirling in me. Within two months Pnina and I and the children left for England, where I was to resume my scholarship for the little

period of time that was left on it. Our ambition had been to
settle in England; I was to look for and hopefully find a job
over the four months that we would be there. In the meantime I continued without relief to live out in my mind the
misery of my loss of Ivana and of Jasmin. So abject did I feel
in my solitary moments, on one occasion I went so far as to
deliberately lay myself down in a flower-bed that was filled
with mud on campus. For what it is worth, a fortune teller,
whom she had consulted, had months before informed Pnina
about how close I was to Jasmin: the fortune teller had said
that Jasmin and I shared a perfect understanding and that
Pnina ought therefore to re-consider the move she was planning for us both and for her children. In the meantime, it was
extremely difficult to make any headway with my thesis from
my study quarters at the university library, for Pnina had
become jealous of my time to myself and would invariably
show up to impose her discontent with my retreating to my
quarters. It was also a time of austerity of a kind I had never
known before, for my scholarship stipend could only have
benefited my wife and my own family; it did not cover the
needs of my new "family," and we were surviving on one bare
meal a day, with rations. In the end I was unable to find
appropriate work, except for the offer of a part-time employ-
ment at a London language school, which could not have
been sufficient for the family's needs, so we were forced to
abandon our unrealistic dream of life in England.

The conditions of our return in themselves constituted
an extraordinary experience. We were in a race against time
imposed upon us by our financial distress. We had elected to
live almost anywhere but in Montreal and had now settled on
Toronto. The trip necessitated our travelling via New York,
whence we would proceed to Toronto by bus. We would be
travelling a good deal, beginning with the two-hour train ride
from Norwich into London and counting the travelling be-

tween one point of arrival to another of departure, and it would be non-stop. I remember feeling a great tunnelling effect at the time, as if powers of destiny were expressing their actual disapproval of our plans to settle in England and the whole idea had been forbidden to us. We eventually arrived in Toronto greatly worn, and needless to say, I was unable to find the kind of job that would allow us to stay, in the greatly shortened time I had, so that we ended up, with a grotesque justice that was obvious to me even then, right back in Montreal, in an acutely small apartment at which my brother had arranged for us to stay for a month at his expense. The apartment was provided with a double-bed only and one dismal window that looked out squarely on a brick wall. The only other peculiar development worth narrating concerning this time is that Pnina's eldest daughter, who was five-and-a-half, would end up, in spite of her knowing next to no English — except, of course, for what she had learned from me — attending the very grade-school *I* had attended in my youth, for about a month, for the apartment my brother had chosen happened to be within the legal precincts of that school.

In a month's time, we finally settled into our own apartment on La Salle Street in Verdun, not too far from the St. Lawrence River. The apartment had three bedrooms and comfortably fitted a family with two young girls and my own study needs. In the meantime I had found work, through my old friend André, as a waiter at the notorious Dunn's Delicatessan. André had long since returned to Montreal and had more or less appropriated the place as its manager, having in his typical way completely won over to his confidence the restaurant's owner, Mr. Dunn himself. On Fridays and Saturdays I worked the overnight shifts till five in the morning, serving customers who had been turned out from the bars, which closed between two and three. They were the shifts during which I accrued most of my weekly revenues. The only veritable satisfaction I derived from that mundane job came when I was let out in the very early hours on those weekend mornings, for I would invariably seek out some impecunious vagrant on the street and pour all the excess change I had collected, short of quarters, into that person's hands, like some newly found treasure, and I recall on one such instance a very moving salutation of overwhelming thanks shouted out to me very loudly all the way down the long strip of Ste. Catherine Street, which at that hour was largely deserted, long after I had stepped away from the vagrant, when he realized just how much of a treasure he felt he had been given. Little did he know, of course, that I myself had fallen quite as low.

I was eventually to leave waiting on tables to become a language teacher once again, working for far better pay within the YMCA Continuing Education Program in down-town Montreal, which at that time had become a burgeoning program and was among the very best in the city. In this period, to my sudden relief, I finally found it in me to piece together the missing links in my thesis that had escaped me. The thesis was now virtually written, though I could not yet realize what this meant, for, first, it would take an entire year to draft the thesis into a form suitable for typing, from all the scattered bits and pieces of writing I had accumulated over many, many months of displaced work. Also, the thesis would not, thanks to my dilatoriness and the other distrac-tions of my life at this time, be fully typed up for submission for yet another year after that.

There followed a time of relative peace in our lives that would continue for two full years. Our first summer of peace was genuinely splendid in its own way. What I especially recall were our romantic efforts to deliberately beautify the lives of the children, an effort symbolically reflected in the very way we dressed them, though to some that effort might have seemed overly self-conscious. In styles of dress that I picked out and Pnina cut and sowed, as well as in their dress hats dramatically adorned with long ribbons, the children might have seemed like several versions of Madeline. We must have been quite a sight in our strolls: a young couple in their late twenties (though we appeared younger) with three girls — for Jasmin would join us on our afternoon perambulations on weekends. This was the time when the three were coming to terms with what it meant to be born in the age of the "new" family: remarkably enough, among themselves, there was to be an overwhelming acceptance and intense excitement about each other. A second daughter, whom Pnina and I had named Paloma after Picasso's daughter, had been born to me in late April. Paloma was especially stunning in her extremely blond hair that seemed almost white.

One experience on our leisurely outings stands out for me as especially reflective of that time. Over the previous winter we had once been out to the house of my close friend, Eric (he who had once remarked on Ivana as "a creature of light"), and while we were dining on that occasion, Eric had made his association with the Anthroposophy of Rudolf Steiner known to Pnina. It seems that Pnina had heard of this Movement while back in Israel, and the revelation that came from meeting up with an anthroposophist of some ten years standing in a person of such dignity as Eric had overwhelmed her with a desire to plunge into the reading of Steiner. I had had a number of short expositions of what Anthroposophy involved from Eric before then — when I was still at university in Montreal, but I had never undertaken a reading of Steiner for myself. Now, however, I began to hear more about Steiner's work and revelations, from Pnina, who had become a voracious reader of the work from the first, and one account of Steiner's I noted with special attention. It had to do with Schubert, who was known to have had one great outburst of violent anger in his life. It occured as he was coming away from a performance of Racine's *Iphigenie.*

Someone he was with had remarked negatively on Racine's play, and Schubert had been offended to the point of an intense physical attack on the other man. It would have been altogether unheard of in the exquisitely sweet, romantic and pacific Schubert, but, on the basis of the studies in Karma and Reincarnation to which Steiner had been led after an extraordinary lifetime devoted to spiritual research, Steiner would maintain that the violence had erupted from Schubert out of the unconscious memory of his former life as a Moorish warrior. Among other things Steiner maintained that Schubert owed the very quality of his distinctive romantic strain in music to his former life in that richly sensuous culture.

Hearing of this struck a deep chord in me, and it led me to wonder about my own exposure to an Arab experience — not just in Ahmad, who had been the best man at my wedding to Ivana, but also now, more subtly, in Pnina's own children who were born of a Moroccan father. This exposure had struck me as linked in the present instance also with the East European influence that had generally come into my life in this period. This influence I now saw in my imagination in part as an outgrowth of that Arab past, as I believe it is in respect of the gypsy strain in that cultural area. Not least remarkable, of course, was how this East European influence, which had now virtually claimed my life, had been preluded for me in the music of Schubert himself. However that may be, an experience occured, while Pnina and I and the children were out on one of our numerous strolls, which haunted me to the very depths of my being.

We were on that occasion in Angrignon Park — at that time our most cherished haunt. It was late one summer evening, and the sun had long gone down, when on our long stroll out of the park, the air was suddenly pierced by the

passionate wailing of a young Arab man who had started up
in this glorious strain out of the camp of family picknickers
who regularly collected round the grills where food was
cooked. Arrested by the sound, I had turned back on our way
out to look and could identify the group out of which the
singer's voice resounded, which continued with an un-
abashed transparency. Suddenly the entire park on that side
had been transpierced with the air of this proud distressful
chanting, as if this Arab youth could only ever be where he
was culturally meant to be, though presently only in some
park in Montreal. He was back, that is, in his own homeland,
around some re-invigorating camp fire, perhaps where warri-
ors gathered looking for relief in the night to soothe them all
amidst the horrible despoilings of war.

*

This was to be a period in which music would again penetrate
my life profoundly. Paloma herself was at the center of much
of the listening I did at this time. Often, when I sat down to
listen, I would place her on my knees, moving her exactly to
the sweep and sway of the music's many diverse rhythms. I
had gotten concentrated more intensely than ever before on
chamber music: the piano trios of Schubert, as well as his
Trout Quintet, the violin-and-piano pieces of Beethoven, the
piano trios of Mozart, his piano quartets and piano quintet,
the piano quartet and piano quintet of Schumann, Schubert's
late quintet, of course. Listening to that music at the time
seemed just the right thing for the extremely small, yet intimate quarters of the living room that lay at the center of our
apartment on La Salle. This room was cut off from any view
of the outside, except for a window that looked out on a
cramped square at the center of the building itself, along with
all the other apartments — above, below and across: the

apartments would otherwise have been altogether bricked in at the center. To compensate for this complete restriction, except for some light that creeped down into the apartment from above, I had set a delicate art deco lamp atop my great mahogany table that had followed me there; the table itself took up almost half the room and had almost the look and feel of a piano in our midst, especially when the lamplight was shining over it.

Paloma had an especially developed interest in the music I played. Some time later, when I had added Verdi's *Rigaletto* to our repertoire, because of the intense father-daughter theme it contains, and when Paloma was old enough to be walking, it became her habit (especially when she had just woken up) to ask expressly to listen to that piece, which she would refer to with authority as "La-la." On those occasions, it became a ritual of mine to set a sort of fool's cap on her head with a bell at the end of it, and she would never vouchsafe to let us listen to that piece without first making sure that the hat was on her. She had become the delight of my days.

*

In our second summer as a family, I was to return for a brief stay to my family country place in the Laurentians, for the first time since the late spring of that year when I was working on the Manitt volume and anguishing over my separation from Judit. Of course Pnina and the children came along, but Jasmin did not join us on that occasion. It was Paloma's first time on our family's country ground, and she was especially stunning crawling about in her sun-white blond hair under those tall pine trees that her great-grandfather had planted so many years before — like some flashing, angelic child-sprite dropped down at the foot of our ancestral grove. At some point during our stay, we had all gotten out on the lake in a rowboat, and I remember Pnina remarking, not long after I had taken the oars to row us along, that *there* I had come into my native element: the aura of those fine hills and lake, so resonant with my deepest self, hung all about me once again. Yet in spite of Pnina's ability to share in the depth of the impression nature made on me in general, and that sacred spot in particular, she remained along with her own children somehow quite apart from it, as if that whole scene were not anything they could ever really know, accustomed as they were, one might suppose in their very blood, to another cultural setting and another natural environment. I myself could successfully penetrate their own cultural ethos in some significant way, due to that instinctive imagination for all things European that had been ingrained so powerfully in me especially from the time of my encounter with Judit. It was also in my very nature to be able to open up to the ethnic quality of other peoples — a capacity that made me ideally suited for my work as a teacher of English as a Foreign Language. But it was clear that Pnina and the children were unable to share freely in my own culture. Here their imagination was limited, and I was forced to recognize what I had never encountered before in those otherwise close to me: an aliennness of nature that at bottom insisted on its own things only. To this attitude I attribute my insurpassable difficulty in finally relating with Pnina's children or with Pnina herself, who always remained in their cultural spirit, in some unspoken part of themselves, wilfully apart from me.

This attitude was positively encouraged by the children's father who, feeling threatened by the influence I would have on the children with Pnina during the week, would invariably work on their spirits on weekends to the point of their complete discouragement on their return to us. Faced with this counter-influence from the father from week to week, we seemed unable to evolve, while on the other side of the situation, there was Pnina's constant resentment of Jasmin, in whom Pnina saw the mere shadow of her own children and an unsatisfactory cultural influence from her side. It became clear to my deepest self that Paloma alone held this culturally impossible situation together — as the daughter to us both, and the sister to all three others. It was she who held virtually all our separate cultures in herself, though everyone else would have to suffer from a perpetual tug of war. There the center would not hold, and one scene I remember from this time, of much pathos now that I look back, concerns Paloma who, seeming to understand the strain that had entered the family, though she was barely two, had come upon the image she needed to express herself. I had taken her out for a walk around the buildings that lined the south side of La Salle to an efflux of the St. Lawrence River — I was standing on a mound of sand looking down at the river at my feet, while I held Paloma in my arms. It was a brisk day in late spring, and there lying before us were two empty rowboats, moored and lying at some distance from each other in the water, though the boats were, strangely, also bound to each other with an iron chain. It was altogether astonishing to hear Paloma, at the sight of these boats, suddenly pronounce the words: "Mummy — Daddy."

*

My growing despair in this period continued, however, and was heightened by the fact that I had had to give up my study to make way for a bedroom for the eldest. There were a number of efforts to find me a room at the cheapest price in some boarding house nearby where I might be able to carry on my literary work with some privacy, but the idea came to naught. On occasion I would take to roaming the streets in the area to get away, and on one such peregrination earlier in the winter I ended up standing before a church that had impressed me by its stark structure, so reminiscent of the world of Yeats, especially with its prominent bell tower, unlike anything I had seen before in a church in Montreal. As it turned out, this was the Irish parish of St. Willibrord's Church, and here I would return on a few other dark evenings, in the spirit of my desolation "to trace/Enthralled by the unconquerable delusion,/Magical shapes" — impelled, that is, by some vain hope that I might yet be delivered of my distress. On another occasion my peregrinations had led me farther down the St. Lawrence River to the west at the point where the river biforcates before the Île des Soeurs. I had laid myself down in the tall grass on the river side, overwhelmed once again with the hopelessness I was feeling, when I was suddenly absorbed by a faint sound that might have been coming out of my own mind and was growing louder. It was the sound of a motor boat going by very slowly on the river. A tall man with sun-glasses was confidently standing in the boat, looking out directly at *me* with a penetrating intensity, as if he might be privy to my deepest feelings, and at that moment it struck me that here was an apparition as it were out of my future, as if the man might be speaking to me, out of some deep meditative center, of my return from the deathly sphere into which I had fallen.

In July of our third summer together as a family, we moved into an apartment not far away from the spot where I had had the vision of the man in the boat. I had discovered the apartment on one of my many strolls in that area. The apartment being somewhat larger, I would have an entire study room to myself, in the front part that overlooked the river. The view of the river going by, so quietly and surely, from that third storey perch, was heart-warmingly splendid, and this was indeed to be a glorious summer. There was a

particular spot by the other shore, which I could focus from
the apartment, that especially captivated my attention at that
time, for there in a small cove the river seemed as it were to
come to a standstill, it made an impression of such deep
peace, and I remember associating the effect that this spot
made on me expressly with the spirit of nature in which I had
become absorbed from my reading at that time, which consisted of *Thus Spake Zarathustra* and *Faust*. In those days the
grasses by the river were allowed to grow tall, and on many a
summer evening these became royally bathed with the golden-red light of the sun that was setting just behind us: the
entire sky opposite would reflect that light in great swirls of
cloud formations, in innumerable textures of color that did
not cease to keep us in awe. Over the course of that sky on
many an evening over that summer a great solitary falcon
would often be spotted by one or other of us, making its
powerful, graceful way back from one of its typical peregrinations to the great common reserve of falcons that was to be
found not far from where we lived, over to the west.

On her visits with us over that refulgent summer Jasmin
seemed especially radiant and fulfilled, transfigured by surroundings that seemed to speak deeply to her also. The children seemed indeed to be more satisfied than ever before, free
as they were to roam at play in the grasses and by the river,
under my watchful eye. Evenings would be a time in which
we would take our walk as a family along the river, using for
this purpose a dirt road that at that time bordered the river,
going east. Clusters of purple spike and other river flowers
culled by the children lined the road on the side of the river,
while the tall golden-red grasses sloped down towards us
from above on the other side. The nature which Pnina and I
shared so profoundly from the first seemed over this period
to have in this way come to fruition all around us. However,
things between us were never what they might have been —

the strain in our relationships on every hand remaining, in spite of the glory all around us, and one incident, on looking back I find to be the symbolic straw that would finally break my camel's back.

It was on the occasion of a visit by Pnina's parents from Israel. Pnina's eldest daughter had been sitting with her nearest sister and with Pnina's father in the sand in a playground not far from the apartment, and I had come out to let them know that dinner was ready. At the sight of my appearance from a distance, this eldest daughter had in her excitement spontaneously risen, with the intention of running out to greet me, when her grandfather put out his arm to restrain her and sit her down again — as if she need not and should not be displaying that kind of excitement with me. There was also a new attitude in Pnina that was isolating her more and more in her own experiences of mind, the result of her growing absorption in the anthroposophy she was now reading with a fanatical insistence before which everything else had become secondary. She had also begun to attend study meetings among anthroposophists. Already she was pursuing a direction of life that seemed no longer to allow for equal and open communications between us.

Once again, an inner image of this time presented itself to me in an outer occurrence. An unhooded woman, in shades of dark brown and grey, had begun to make her appearance on the open ground that lay just above that point where the hill of grasses sloped down towards the river. In her walking back and forth on this ground almost every evening, she seemed to be continually at prayer, and in her solitariness, and in her sombreness, she cut a figure that only became more and more impressive as the summer wore on. Among other things at this time, I remember taking Paloma down to the river regularly in the late evening just before it was time to put her to bed; I would carry her to the river in my arms in her nightwear, and there, before the river, I would intone on her behalf, and my own, the prayer I knew so well from Eliot's *Ash-Wednesday:*

> Spirit of the river, spirit of the sea . . .
> let my cry come unto thee . . .

*

It was also in this period that I introduced myself to Father Joseph Cameron of St. Willibrord's Church, in the parish of which we now lived. The very first time I attended there, I was overwhelmed with the power of his spirit, which spoke, whether at homily or when officiating, with a voice of authority that might have belonged to Ralph Waldo Emerson. When I heard Joe Cameron on that first occasion, he had only just recently lost his mother, having stopped at the start of his homily to thank his parishioners for their condoling support, but, though it was obvious that he was still grieving, the full force of his imaginative spirit seemed only the more transfigured from that death. I had attended morning mass on a few occasions and had offered to be of help if there were any need, but I had then left off going for a while, only to get a call from Cameron one afternoon to say that he missed my presence.

I would, not long after that, invite Joe Cameron over to our home, in whose somewhat cramped quarters he cut a powerful figure. Pnina could not help remarking that the man seemed a tower of strength. On that same occasion, I would take a very long walk with him along the river, going west for some distance, in spite of the very brisk cold of that late November day. I remember the wind blowing very hard and cold upon us, and I had stopped Cameron along the way to inquire of him how it was that he could speak with such power and authority, and he had in that moment simply bowed his head to the ground at his feet — he was dressed in that distinctive knitted winter cap of his with the flaps over his ears and the loose strings that blew freely in the wind — and he had very simply said, through eyes that watered from the cold, that it was all the work of "The Spirit."

*

Two months after that encounter I would move out into my own apartment on Verdun Street, one back window of which looked out squarely to the northwest on the cupola of St. Joseph's Oratory, which showed just over the mountain. From my contact with Joe in this period I had suddenly felt all the power I needed to come back to my own self after years of being adrift in turmoil, confident now in my right to the purity of my self, after being mired in so much pulling and tearing for so long. The room with the view of St. Joseph's I would deck out fully for Paloma, who came to visit twice a week, and Jasmin too would be free to visit me there. However, it was, for all that, a period of great trial — to find myself alone, for the first time in my life, in that darkest time of the year (for this was early January); the self-emptying I went through then was appalling, and it was only to be relieved (in that purest way, in which we seem ideally intended to find relief), through the intense light of religious devotion. It seems altogether appropriate that in that first January I should attend an amazing celebration held on the feast day of the Epiphany in the main Chapel of the old Mother House of the Congregation of Notre Dame, on Sherbrooke Street near Atwater.

It was to be the very last celebration of its sort, for the glorious Mother House had been sold and would soon be converted to make way for its new function as Dawson College at the end of that year. I remember the archbishop stopping at some point in his homily to make reverential reference to the House's hallowed walls of many generations' standing, and I remember a great effusion of intensest devotion and light among the crowds of CND nuns who were all in attendance that day to commemorate the history of their order. All seemed, in spite of the sad farewell to an old era, altogether in tune with their faith in the "light in the east" that the Magi themselves had followed — that light that is said to have shone out in the darkness. I had the very special experience at that time of being personally connected with one of these CND nuns who worked at Willibrord's parish as Joe's immediate assistant. I had been coupled with her in a prayer group I had been attending there since before Christmas — Sr. Clare O'Neill was her name. I was in awe of the exquisite tenderness and the utter perfection of fellow feeling (the tenderness of a compassion that actively worked its magic) that Clare continually bestowed upon us, as she generously shared with us her sense of the spiritual will our group was desperately seeking. It was all too easy to believe that she indeed carried in herself the spirit of her favorite gospel of St. Luke, just as Joe Cameron carried in himself the spirit of the gospel of St. John. It was the beginning of what was to be my longstanding relationship to St. Willibrord's parish, though it would take time to break the ice.

*

In the meanwhile, I had become greatly absorbed in the idea of Orpheus, over the many afternoons I spent that winter in the graduate study room tucked away in a remote corner of the fifth floor of the deceprit old Norris Building that once served as the Concordia University Library. The study room was hard to find, and those who worked there were invariably committed to intensely silent work, with the advantage also of a window that looked out on a peaceful backyard scene of skylights around which pigeons gathered all the time. There was the added convenience of having the stacks of books ranged just outside the room in the library corridors. It was here, on one of many effortless forays into the stacks, that I came across Elizabeth Sewell's *Orphic Voice*, and I myself began a poem (the only one I ever formally attempted) in free verse, which I entitled "Orphic Prelude." (I never kept track of the poem after that.)

The poem was concentrated on the moment of Orpheus' first entrance into Hell only — hence my idea of a "prelude," and most of the action centered on the guilt of wrong-doing that, in the face of his overpowering impulse to recover his lost Eurydice, I had made the basis of Orpheus' loss and descent into Hell. Strangely enough, I had associated the loss of Eurydice in my mind with my abandonment of Pnina, and it was the river that had figured so prominently in my life in recent years that served as the river on which my Orpheus made his descent. The poem was repeatedly marked, as Orpheus made his way down, with appeals to the Father for blessing, in a confessional mode that brought Joe Cameron into the purview of my imagination, as if the images might have been those of one of my dreams, and the poem continually projected horrid if triumphant visions (out of Ovid) of the final end that seemed yet to capture all the terror of my present dissociation:

> The dead tongue sang; funereally the river banks
>   and reeds
> Echoed their music.
> The head faced upward on strange sands,

Yet one thing it seemed impossible for me to think I or any one else could manage in these circumstances, though the words seemed to be directly addressed to me at this time, and this was the idea that Rilke puts forward so boldly in his *Duino Elegies:*

> Isn't it time that we should lovingly free
> ourselves from the beloved and endure it with trembling:
> as the arrow endures the string, focused in its release
> to be more than itself?

*

Of course my life went on. I had by then fully done filling out Paloma's room with all the playthings I thought she would want to have at hand whenever she visited, and in spite of my overwhelming sense of loss in this period, I would repeatedly experience a kind of rapture in distress that I associated with my reading of Yeats, but also with Mozart whose music I would return to continually at this time. Especially I listened to Mozart's last two symphonies, which formed the basis of my education of Paloma. I had broken the music down into two roles played on the one hand by a princess and on the other by the kingly father who has his daughter's education in mythical power in mind.

Those who have listened to this music will surely identify the two elements I speak of, which I believe are indeed given to us as the gradual initiation of the princess-soul by a mythical kingly power. Nothing invokes the power of the mythical gods of old more strongly for me than do the many movements from these symphonies. One is asked to think of a kingly power slowly gathering in force of revelation; the many aspects of the power he reserves to himself are gradually collected together, and at one point there is expression of power at the more contained level of social-cultural initiation, then, more openly, at the tremendous level of elemental revelation; in the second movement of the 41st Symphony there is also an expression at the level of the initiation of the feelings. The climax to this amazing presentation, than which I believe there is no comparison in any of the arts, is the continuous self-revelation in mythical power which the kingly element accomplishes in the last movement of the 41st Symphony — appropriately enough entitled the "Jupiter" Symphony.

It is as if we were being asked to contemplate with Mozart a power that can only be reborn in greater and greater strength with every new death it seems to undergo: the whole put on without reserve before the princess-soul! What more comprehensive release for me, in the distressing circumstances through which I was passing at this time. When listening to this music, I would point out to Paloma when the princess appeared looking out on the kingly power, and when the king himself showed up, who kept showing her how continually strong he was and how rapturous — assuring her of his care of her with all angels at his command, even though *she* might be watching only as from a distant shore. One movement especially formed a special ritual between us: the third movement from the 40th, which takes the form of a splendid march. It was my habit, when we listened, to get Paloma to march in a carefully measured way to this music as *I* led the way right through the apartment — each of us marking our path before us with a staff in one hand: always in a certain stride that we both had to maintain in keeping with the definite rhythm of the music's progress. It was to be my way of instilling in Paloma the best sense of measure and of strength that I could hope for for her burgeoning soul, for the future life that lay in store for her.

My "education" of Jasmin, on the other side, took a considerably different form befitting her more tender and dreamier nature. With her I listened intently to the pearly dreaminess of the slower, exquisitely tender movements out of Schumann as she lay tucked up in bed on Saturday nights under the glow of that same small rosy lamplight I had kept by her for years. Especially I recall the slower, "singing" movements out of the Piano Quartets No. 44 and 47. I continued of course to read to her out of the fairy tales as of old, but as Jasmin was now in her sixth year, I was also able to bring her those moral lessons which take the form of Aesop's fables. It was in the context of this focus on animals that I introduced her to anthroposophical lore that I had begun to garner from the small reading of anthroposophy I had commenced. I spoke to her of the eagle of thinking, the bull of warm love, the lion of adventure and the man in us who brings all of these things together. What a revelation for Jasmin then to discover as she sat by herself, waiting for me one Sunday morning in one of the church pews at St. Willibrord's (I was reading that day and was sitting separately from her in the sanctuary), that the church ceiling just above the altar area held portraits of that very eagle, bull, lion and man! The very thing she had heard about from me! Who can measure the effect such congruencies of perception can have in the, as yet, unshaped mind of a child? It was the first thing she exclaimed about to me that day when mass was over and she was free to run over to me. And to think she had continued to sit to herself alone with that new vision blooming in her for some time before she could speak of it to anyone. Jasmin had become the darling of the few CND nuns who gathered for worship at Willibrord's arriving from their own Congregation house in the parish, and in time, as a certain perception of their working spirit had grown on her, Jasmin too now wore a small gold cross of her own choosing, which I had gotten for her, over her blouses, and she continued to wear that cross, I was told, even when she was away from me. Jasmin would continue in this way to be my companion for early Sunday mass for many months to come.

*

Paloma's introduction to the parish was of another sort. Always the more active of the two, she had a habit, after all the parishioners had taken their leave of Joe after mass and I was in the position to set her free (she was barely three at the time), to run up eagerly to him, haling him with that typical glee of hers as —"the father in white." This was after the poem by Blake I had been reading to her for months. And it is in fact the season in which Joe wore white that I especially associate with Paloma's time at Willibrord's. I would not be alone in saying that Joe had constantly about him an aura of the resurrection-faith, unlike any I have ever encountered or am ever likely to encounter again in our time. It was the faith around which my life was being transformed. In him one knew, as one learns to know well the most ordinary things of life, that Love of which John speaks that is in process of chasing all darkness away. Joe's power came from an overwhelming capacity for seeing the power of Christ at work in each one of us, so that all were made to feel in every respect His equal: the very Friends whom Christ had addressed and sought in the Gospel of John.

I never encountered a celibrant more capable of bringing his congregation together in deep worship. With his insistence on extending moments of silence during his celebration of the Mass, simply because he could sense that this person or that, this group or the other, was still not attending closely enough — calling us repeatedly to order as it were from one moment to another — we would often find him looking out at us directly while he was engaged in his offices, as if calling us to see for ourselves what he was doing exactly. It was his way of gathering all who were present from their many dissociated states, to ensure that at the right point all would be brought beyond themselves into that perfect other-centered condition that allowed for the kind of entry into the Trans-substantiation that was intended from the beginning. We were made to share in the "breaking of the bread" in the way this is intended at the supper at Emmaus: that is, as something "seen" to be happening through our "breaking forth," beyond the bounds of our worldly egoisms, into that purely *other-centered* consciousness which knows exactly out of what greater Impulse we look upon each other and gather ourselves to each other out of our many respective callings. Joe Cameron worked on in our midst through his constant example. At any moment also during his parochial work — given my own ability to "break forth" on occasion — I felt I had the power to unite with him in the consciousness of the Transubstantiation that is ongoing in every action we accomplish and every movement we make; it was a matter of constantly "seeing" with him, as he went about his own motions and actions. He led us by a pure example, and also by his voice in which this same consciousness was conveyed as a deep tone, so that I had no difficulty whatever in comprehending what is said of the voice of the Good Shepherd:

> And when he putteth forth his own sheep, he goeth before them, and the sheep follow him: for they know his voice.

*

But this is to anticipate the long-term development I would undergo over a close association with Joe that would continue for almost ten years. In the meantime, I had been called to take my oral exam for my Ph.D — within three months of my assuming my own apartment — in March of 1985. I flew back to England to take the exam, which was a success; the trip was otherwise uneventful, except for the fact that I stopped over to visit Owen Barfield at his place in the country of Kent just outside London: Orchard View, as his place was called. Even at eighty-seven Barfield was astonishingly hale, driving me both from and back to the train station through those narrow lanes in the British countryside that are called roads, at a solid speed that was more than daring. Apart from that, I might as well have been in the midst of the countryside around Coleridge's Stowey Cottage as in the romantic countryside in which this great authority on Coleridge had lodged himself. Barfield had become my literary champion from the time I had read his first book, *Poetic Diction*, significantly enough on the occasion of my one and only visit to my family's country-place with Pnina and the children. I had been greatly impressed to discover that here was another who besides myself was ready to attribute to language (at some stage of its development, as well as continuously in many different senses) a literal power to evoke otherworldly realities. Barfield had been lampooned for thinking this by his closest friend, C.S. Lewis, who yet continued to think Barfield the wisest man he had ever known. *Poetic Diction* I realized was the unspoken spirit that had hung over my thesis from the beginning, though I was not to discover the book until the thesis had already been fully written and was more or less typed up, so that I never did have the chance to base my thesis on its content or even to refer to it with much effect (though the thesis does finally contain a quote from the book by way of an epigraph). One might think it had been intended that I should have access to this book only after I had first "proven" myself from research carried out on my own. At any rate, at my interview with Barfield, I was to discover that he had also written *Saving the Appearances*, about which, as he explained to me, he had received a letter from T.S. Eliot, who thought it one of the best books he had read in many years. Needless to say I would turn to this book with a passion on my return from England.

In the meantime I had come to Barfield to share with him what I called a "counter-reality" that I felt at a certain point overwhelms Shakespeare as well as some of his Jacobean contemporaries, as it had formerly overcome Marlowe. In some sense that I thought momentous, I offered the view that these dramatists were *destined* to have the experience of "going under" in the worst possible sense of despair of their souls, what's more, that it would have to be in the terms of their destiny logically to find their way back *out* of a pure despair, and to prove my point, vague though this seemed at the time, I offered to read Faustus' long last speech to Barfield, who was finally greatly moved by the reading. This is the speech in the play when Faustus is finally dragged down to Hell without his power to avert that outcome. I am not sure that the point registered with Barfield in the sense I was trying to convey, but he himself was struck by how powerful that long last speech is, as if he had never quite heard or seen it in its appalling power before. Nothing more came of this discussion, but Barfield's own influence and the influence of his work would hang over me for many years to come and would not bear fruit in my critical work until the publication, over ten years later, of *Othello's Sacrifice,* in 1996.

*

Not long after that milestone visit, I returned to Montreal, a Doctor of Philosophy so-called, or at least soon to be one, but I was not to find work more suitable to those accomplishments until the fall of that year. Uncannily, I was hired on at Dawson College, at the labyrinthine Lafontaine campus on Viger Street, before the big move to the Mother House. I was asked to replace an ailing professor and to continue with his close reading, with his class group, of two long works, appropriately enough in the present circumstances of my life, *Crime and Punishment* and *Don Quixote*. Here was another of those deep uncanny correspondences with the inner development of my life. One episode in *Crime and Punishment* especially I was able to seize upon, with a special effect on my class. It is the episode in which we learn in passing (Dostoyevsky does not emphasize the point as he is going along) that Sonia, Raskolnikov's loving savior, has for some time now been wearing around her neck the cross once worn by the girl whom Raskolnikov felt forced to murder the night he comes upon her unexpectedly in the apartment where he murders the old pawnbroker.

With Raskolnikov we learn from Sonia that she and the girl had been best friends and that they had at one time exchanged crosses, as a sign of their mutual friendship and fidelity. From this, we quickly deduce that in that moment when Raskolnikov brings his axe down on the girl, Sonia's own cross hangs there upon that girl; that is to say, in the very moment when Raskolnikov is throwing his soul away, a saving power, in the form of Sonia, is already *in place*, to protect him from damning himself any further by his deed. My class was especially impressed with the idea of a providential power that could work with such a complete prescience to counteract what would otherwise be a hopeless fate. A still greater thought that passed through my own mind at this time was how it could be in someone's destiny to sacrifice herself in death in order to bring a person she had made her best friend together with another who would never have come to life again spiritually without the gift of that best friend to save him from himself.

*

Over the next two years the course of my life would take a twofold direction. On the one hand, I would start to make some first serious inroads in the reading of Rudolf Steiner's anthroposophy, though I was to begin with some of the most difficult texts, namely *Theosophy* and *The Archangel Michael and the Human Gemut*. I recall reading *Theosophy* in the evenings over the summer of 1985 (of all places) at that very spot by the river that I had long made my own. On one such occasion while I sat there reading, I had (nothing less than) a view of Pnina herself and all the children sitting out on the balcony, taking in the picturesque scene that stood before us all that evening in the sky across the river. It was impossible for me to know who was with them all, though I could see there was another. Two factors had driven me to begin a reading of Steiner. It was a discovery bordering on revelation to learn, as I undertook my reading of *Poetic Diction* that first time in the country, that Owen Barfield, to whose book, by a natural path of development, I had been led in my own literary research, turned out to be a staunch anthroposophist himself. He points out in (a late edition of) this very book that he had owed all of his own ideas, from the very start of his production, to what he claimed was the far greater and original achievement of Rudolf Steiner's anthroposophy, which he had come across in his early twenties. At the same time, I had been incited to begin my own reading from quite another motive stemming from my separation from Pnina. On my leaving her, the feeling had grown in me that I was being left out of a course of development that now associated her with my close an-throposophist-friend Eric. It seemed to me that my own life had been appropriated from me from within as it were, and, as I learned from Eric, Pnina had indeed tried to slander me with him by implying that I was not, and would never be, an anthroposophist. Something, then, of outrage at her attempt to displace me from within my own life, and to deprive me of the possibility of being accepted as an anthroposophist, com-pelled me to take up a reading of Steiner for myself. In the meantime, Pnina was quickly making her way through a number of Anthroposophical Society circles and would soon be living with the man who was generally regarded by the members in Montreal as their leading anthroposophist — a man who was to play a major and decisive role in my own life when I would meet him later, quite apart from the fact that he had become in the meantime a step-father to my daughter. His name was Tibor, an Hungarian with an admirable fluency in English, among anthroposophists that I have met capable of the most extraordinary thinking I have ever encountered.

*

However, my own direction would take me for the moment along another route. After a full year of teaching at Dawson College, I was in the position in the summer of 1986 to turn my attention to working over some of my thesis-material for the first time for publication. The result would be a first article on "Sexuality in *Hamlet*" (to be later drafted as the second chapter of my first book), an article that would remain one of my most self-defining pieces as a critic, accepted by *Hamlet Studies* in February of 1987. Just how it came about that I found myself working at this piece for purposes of publication — what force it was that could possibly rouse me back, after a gap of almost four years, to a certain faith in the work I had done and could do — all this remains as deep a mystery to me as the force that suddenly rouses Hamlet back to the sense of his own destiny when he is adrift at sea. Other matters had absorbed me over those years that seemed to me far more urgent: my "struggle" with my new "family", primarily. My association with Joe at Willibrord's and my active participation in the Church accounted for the other main direction in my life at this time.

In the fall of 1986 I was to meet, in this Church context, two of the most creative human souls I am ever likely to meet. One was an English teacher in high school who had come away from his time as a seminarian to re-consider the direction he wished to take with his life. His name was Peter Kelly, an Irishman, no more than five years older than myself, whose way of magically engaging the spiritual warmth of those around him was indescribable. One could well believe that he might be intended to bring the warmth of spiritual life to others in an official pastoral role of some kind, but it was clear that he wished to share in the creation of that spiritual life more openly and freely, out in the world. He had brought his talents for music to Willibrord's, ready to be recruited as a Church minstrel, for he was a powerful singer who also played the guitar. In the meantime, another remarkable soul had found her way back to Willibrord's. Her name was Terry. She had returned, after ten years of missionary work abroad in Japan as a member of the congregation of CND nuns, to the parish in which she had grown up.

She too had been an English teacher, but, as is the custom in that world, her congregation had decided to call her back, after so long a period of work, for another, fresh assignment. Being forced to return from her life with the Japanese had not sat well with Terry, especially as she had formed many close attachments to that Oriental people, of whom she had become very fond. The time she was to spend at Willibrord's would in consequence be on the whole distressful for her, because of all she had had to forsake. She was especially overcome, as I recall, on one particular occasion, having learned of the sudden death of an Oriental man for whom she had retained the kind of fondness I speak of, and there was a moment in Church — it was some time after service when almost everyone had left — when, in her distress of that death, this dynamic servant of Christ had felt the need to lay herself in my own arms for comfort. It was a moment of indescribable poignancy.

*

Terry was assigned to Willibrord's as Joe's new assistant after Clare O'Neill had been called away to another function herself. Like Peter, Terry was but a few years older than I was, so that for the first time while at Willibrord's I found myself closely related to people of my own generation — Joe, like Clare, being twenty years older, belonged to another generation. So that, if I thought of Joe and Clare as my spiritual father and mother, Peter and Terry became to me my spiritual brother and sister. It is Terry who had recruited Peter to sing with her at Church, and we would soon after form a group of three, singing, for the most part in three-part harmony, a full range of poignantly beautiful songs, among which I remember one in particular set to David's words from one of the Psalms:

> Like a deer that yearns for running streams,
> So my soul is yearning for Thee, My God.
> My soul is yearning for the Lord.
> When shall I see Him face to face?

Until then I had been, under Joe's guidance, a regular Church reader and continued thus. To be proclaiming the Word through my formal reading of the epistles of Paul — among other texts — already constituted a deep and sophisticated and highly privileged spiritual life. However, I was to go through a transformation of soul more immediately miraculous when I found myself over an entire Church season — from Advent to Pentecost — singing together and worshiping so closely with two of the tenderest souls I could know, who had become to me the essence of what a young creative spiritual warmth could accomplish, which seemed to know no bounds.

*

The Easter I went through with Peter and Terry that year was to be the most dramatically satisfying I have ever known. With them I went through the Events of the Passion and Death and Resurrection of Christ with a creative intensity unlike any I have been able to conceive since. It was the great Spring of 1987, as I was to call it: even Joe seemed to sense something altogether extraordinary in the air that year. It was the only Easter celebration in my recollection at which, on taking leave of his congregation, he had pronounced the fateful words: "And may this Easter be the best you have ever known." There seemed to be an especially great burgeoning and sprouting of rich, luscious vegetation that spring, which I seem to recall coming early, and it seems to have been always very splendidly bright and warm. It was in this very time that I met and was soon to fall in love with a woman only a year younger than myself, of stunning magical beauty — a native of Montreal who was also a Russian Ashkenazy Jew. Her name was Marilyn. Very fair, she had eyes that overpowered one religiously with their soft blue magic. It was to be a time of deep spiritual romance and also of overwhelmingly intense magical sexuality, which I would associate to a great extent with the wonder of Marilyn's small apartment on St. Marc Street (at 1439) in downtown Montreal, which became a kind of shrine to me.

I remember returning occasionally to that door on my own, long after our time together there, looking in from the foyer at that fine, large dark-wood apartment door No. 3 that separated me from what had been for me an initiation site, nothing less. The place was made special by the fact that here was a glamorously good-looking young woman living happily on her own in the very heart of the city, and yet this was the quietest apartment I had ever been in, made so by the fact that it lay farther to the back of the apartment building than did the other apartments, looking out on a square ground that was overgrown with weeds and remained unkept, so that no one ever stepped out into that backyard. The place was boxed in from the city streets on every side, with the result that one heard but a continuous faint humming of traffic coming to us from over the tops of the buildings. It was a place quiet as no place could be on any side street in any district in the rest of the city, and I especially remember waking up to Marilyn in the morning in late spring of that year to the warm, bright light outside that beige, flowered curtain that fluttered so quietly above the window that had been left open over the course of the night, thinking that we might just as well be out alone in the country as in the heart of a city, for the deep magical peace of that remarkable setting.

The spring of 1987 was to be astounding in far more ways than one. It was also at this time that I got to meet Tibor, after several visits to Paloma's new home at the extreme other side of the city, on Laval Island. In spite of Pnina's treatment of me on our first separating from each other, I had managed to remain aloof from the injury to ensure Paloma's well-being, and I often allowed myself to be invited into Paloma's new home to her great pride and joy. Pnina continued in her overbearing spiritual attitudes, which she thought made her greatly knowing and greatly superior to me; it was her own work, I knew, that had set Tibor in the role of a kind of kingly cult hero as he spoke from the long, very high-backed wicker chair with rounded arms that he sat on every time he held his intimate group-sessions in Anthroposophy in the basement of their suburban home. I was privileged to attend on occasion, and, ignoring the cultish aura of that setting, I was over-

whelmed with the structural power and logic of Tibor's thinking which I knew he had successfully extended into the
spheres of esoteric consciousness about which Anthroposophy speaks.

If anyone had won me over to Anthroposophy now, it
was Tibor himself, for Pnina's association with it, and indeed
even Eric's, had until then struck me as the interest of a form
of sub-culture — quite wrongly, as I look back, but it remains
true that I knew at that time of no other basis that connected
Anthroposophy more objectively to the world at large.
Pnina's injury to my person had motivated me negatively: I
felt the need to come to terms with Anthroposophy as an
unknown quantity of thought and experience that, if I did not
master for myself, would, I felt, continue to subvert me as a
mocking influence in my life. Barfield's own association with
Anthroposophy had opened to me, as powerfully as any great
literary standing could, the links to it from Literature, but no
personal influence of any kind had passed from him to me at
our interview, so that I felt no special confirmation of the
value of the pursuit from his source, and indeed Barfield
himself stood out in the world at that time as a lone and
unregarded champion of Steiner. His own presentation of
Anthroposophy (in *Romanticism Comes of Age*) had struck me
as overly reticulate and too theoretically ingrown for me to
feel the case for its overwhelming relevance to the world from
that demonstration either.

On the other hand, Tibor's capacity for linking his own
thinking so fully and directly to the material of Steiner's
Anthroposophy confirmed my deepest perception of the firm
structure and logic of thinking itself, and to see this function
of the mind so clearly applied in the Anthroposophy practised
by Tibor was decisive in winning me over to Anthroposophy's
unmistakable universality. To this singular capacity (which
apart from Steiner I have encountered in a sustained form

only in the anthroposophist writer, Sergei O. Prokofieff) Tibor
brought, what's more, a depth and sincerity of brotherly love
that served as an additionally strong source of personal motivation, and I can confidently say that of all people I have
known from my past, it is Tibor for whom I reserve a love that
continues to this day unworn and undissipated by time or his
young death (at forty-nine) at an early stage of our relationship.

All things were coming together for me at this time. That
spring I had learned from Tibor of an extraordinary cycle of
lectures given by Steiner in the last phase of his life, which
goes by the title *Symphony of the Creative Word*. It was the most
fitting material for me to be reading in this very special time
of life, for in this cycle Steiner offers us one of his most
concrete and comprehensive accounts of the great interweav-
ing work of the spiritual beings who lie behind the ordering
of Nature and the planetary Cosmos, ranging over the whole
world of minerals, plants, animals and Man. It represented a
highpoint of sorts to be meditating this profound material,
sitting on Marilyn's couch with the door to the backyard open
in the mornings after she had left for work, and with the great
Sun of that extraordinary time warming and illuminating
everything about. Somewhat dramatically, someone had
painted above the tall weeds on the far wall that ran perpendicular to Marilyn's bedroom the colorful word *Braziland* —
which to this day rings to my haunted ears and appears to my
haunted eyes like the great password to some esoteric magical
realm.

No words could describe the luxurious quality of that
grace-filled time that Marilyn and I experienced, for the most
part consciously immersed in nature. It was a quality of grace
that also seemed inscribed in the very ethos of her neighborhood and that apartment. Perhaps the quality I speak of was
to be explained in part as a spiritual "overflow" (so I specu-

lated later) from the Freemason activities that took place at the
Great Hall just up St. Marc on Sherbrooke Street, also from the
Seminary life that continued undiminished after generations
of devotion, beyond the great stone wall just across Sherbrooke Street from the Freemason Hall. (To this Seminary, in
fact, Peter would return a few years later as part of another
unsuccessful attempt to make himself into a priest. Terry for
her part would later become the vice-Principal of a college in
New York State that welcomed students from abroad, and she
would stay on in this capacity even after she was again called
back to Montreal by her Congregation, this time preferring to
leave the order than give up her role among foreigners.) No
doubt the miraculous self-transformation I had been through
at Willibrord's along with Peter, with Terry and with Joe —
Clare too had played her magnificent part — would have
contributed profoundly to the "visionary gleam" that now
spread itself over everything, seemingly without bounds. Anthroposophy and Tibor's influence were also adding their
great contributory waters, and there can be no doubt that all
was indeed coming together for me, far beyond what my poor
self could fully comprehend, or control.

Not least of all was the influence of Marilyn's magical
person, which from the first was associated in my mind inextricably with her Jewishness. There was in her very sexuality
an ultra-precious sanctity that had opened my astonished
imagination to the sacred power that still lay contained in that
great race in which the Christ Himself had incarnated. Also in
that indefinable religious romantic look of hers, so steeped in
a sensual perfection, I could divine, as I often said to Marilyn
herself at the time, the very look that Christ might have had
as He set about gathering His followers to Him, who would
have had no choice but to follow. How strange that the
Christian visionary experience into which I was born at that
time should now be coming to a focus in this Jewish woman

of the most extraordinary beauty and rare destiny. The anomaly was poignantly formulated for us both in the fact that I continued to wear my cross necklace for much of our time together, though this formality of the cross I would shed in time.

Within three months of my meeting Marilyn I had sold most of my furniture to an auctioneer (with the exception of my bookcase and a replica of the bust of Hypnos that I had had with me for years), and I had moved out into a large, ornately designed room in the Victorian home of an Hungarian family of whom I was to grow very fond, just outside Montreal in the city of Westmount (just around the corner from Atwater and Ste. Catherine). The move had been inspired by Marilyn's own choice of living in the heart of the city. Of course one has to work hard at finding the quiet corner one needs sheltered just away from the city hubbub, though it is astonishing how so much quieter it can be when one finds such a place than on any so-called quiet street in the outlying neighborhoods. Something of Marilyn's extraordinary spiritual power, if not a great deal of it, I felt I could attribute to the extraordinary kind of work she did. She was Head of the Recreation Department at the Jewish Hospital of Hope, which at that time was still situated on Sherbrooke Street far out in the east end of the city. This was a chronic care hospital instituted for both Jewish and non-Jewish folk whose remaining time on earth was counted. Marilyn offered her magically intense care to these people as their "angel," as they called her, and, now that I was living downtown myself and had far easier access than previously to any other spot in the city, it became convenient for me to ride down on occasion in the late afternoon on the city's subway to the extreme other end of town to the Hospital at which Marilyn worked. In this way I became intimately familiar with that extraordinary setting, and in time I was visiting some of the patients.

The "angelic" impression Marilyn made in the corridors
of that hospital (she always wore an immaculately white
blouse) was more than stunning, especially as one was surrounded in that context with such devastating images of
human suffering. Many if not all were suffering from some
advanced form of multiple sclerosis or were paralyzed from
some other severe reason or other. One such patient, Rita, was
no longer able to shape words or to move much of her body
at all, though she retained all her intellectual senses and could
hear well enough. I had been told that she had written poetry
and was fond of painting, and I would occasionally visit her
with Paloma, who had barely turned five, to lighten Rita's
mood with some of Paloma's own marvellous drawings or
with some of the songs Paloma had learned from me (one of
which was the hymn to St. Marguerite, set to music by Han-
del, that the CND congregation had made their theme song).
Another patient, Jack, could not move any part of his body,
not even his head, as if he might be fixed in stone, though he
certainly retained feeling and would regularly be found tearing. I recall especially the time I was introduced to him by
Marilyn and I stuck my hand out to his face to caress him in
overwhelmed compassion and amazed pride at the extent of
his suffering. Marilyn was unused to such readiness to acknowledge patients whom for the most part, she said, others
refrained from touching because of a taboo about their dis-
ease. In time, I was to be assigned my own patient, Lise,
whom Marilyn had expressly picked out for me in her typical
social wisdom, for Lise was one of the few non-Jewish resi-
dents at the Hospital, a Catholic and a Quebecoise.

The General, as I called her, she had a remarkably proud
way of holding her head when receiving attention, and she
was entirely possessed of her faculties of mind and speech,
though she was paralyzed from the neck down. From what I
could gather from hints she let fall, she had been pushed

down a staircase by her husband some years back but very strangely did not seem to hold that against him, or at least showed no sign of bitterness at all, a show of courage and spirit that had overwhelmed me in its unspeakable grandeur. In my visits to her, I would often sing her some of the songs I had learned as part of our singing-group at Willibrord's, and especially I recall singing two songs: "Behold the wood of the Cross" (a Good Friday number) and "Send forth your Spirit, O Lord, and renew the face of the earth" (the latter sung at Pentecost and based on one of David's Psalms). Especially there was an indescribable richness to those times when a good number of the patients would be taken out onto the backyard hospital grounds where there was a garden and a picnic area with benches for visitors. On those balmy, sun-filled afternoons, under the tall oak trees that overhung the whole area providing all the shade that these weakened patients needed, I could at leisure watch Marilyn in her blond hair and white shirt moving cheerfully amongst them, as she ceaselessly attended to their needs, their own hair being lightly blown about by the soft breezes, as they sat immobilized in their wheelchairs. It was a scene at which one could feel at once all the agonizing sadness but as well the unspeakable grandeur and beauty of the lives that continued courageously to be lived there.

*

One other area of experience served to round out this climactic moment in my life. It had to do, at the other extreme from chronic suffering, with the fresh youthful life of the children at Willibrord's parish. Not long after I had been recruited to form a singing-group with Peter and Terry, Terry, noticing the intensity of my care of Paloma and my close attachment to young children generally, conceived the notion of my putting on a Christmas play with some of the children from the parish. She knew of my background in Shakespeare, feeling that that might especially qualify me for the work, so she thought. Certainly she had shown great personal vision of me in supposing that such a venture might be the very activity I was seeking, to rouse myself from my melancholy solitude at that time, for this was months before the great Spring, as I continue to call it, when I had yet to find my hard way back from the abyss into which I had fallen. It would take some persuading to bring the women who had formerly been in charge of the Christmas event over to the idea that the children could indeed manage the stage action I projected or the kind of projection that speaking lines in church would require (it was their view that the children would just have to use microphones, that they would need prompting, that they would have to read the lines). In the end I had my way, but only because I had been put in charge. What I learned from the experience was how fully capable even young children could be when encouraged in a sense of pride of their responsibilities, and how overly protective these women had been of such children.

The production turned out a complete success. The children ranged from four to ten, but I had made judicious use of the older children as guides and leaders to the younger, the older children playing the lead roles, the younger serving in a fairly large group as the Chorus. The role of the narrator itself was taken over by a young girl. The Willibrord's sanctuary had staircases descending into the nave at both extremes as well as in the middle, a setting that made for the possibility of an interesting movement from those extreme points, where the Chorus took its place, to the middle where the Holy Family would appear. Standing by the side of the altar (as in many sculptural representations) stood an angel, with a candle. The play I wrote was simple enough, yet effective, and ran as follows:

> *An Angel stands with its back to the side of the altar, holding a lit candle.*
> *On the central staircase that descends from the sanctuary to the nave, on separate steps counting from the first step down, each positioned below the other, the 1st Shepherd stands dead center, the 2nd Shepherd and 3rd Shepherd to each side.*
> *At the bottom of the staircase, well out into the nave of the Church, Herod sits, his head in his knees, a crumpled figure in black.*
> *Darkness, except for background light from the sanctuary and the candlelight held by the Angel.*

1ST SHEPHERD
There are no stars in the sky tonight . . . and it's cold . . .

2ND SHEPHERD
Cold . . .

3RD SHEPHERD
And we have lost our way...

> *From the staircases at the side, in darkness.*

CHORUS
WE HAVE LOST OUR WAY!

1ST SHEPHERD
Where *are* our sheep?

2ND SHEPHERD
What if one of our sheep should be lost!

3RD SHEPHERD
How sad, if one of our sheep should be lost.

CHORUS
HOW SAD!

1ST SHEPHERD

We need a light that will always shine, like the Sun in the East!

As he says this, the Shepherd turns towards the altar to be met by the Angel with candlelight who has stepped out of her place to take up her position at the top of the staircase.

As the Shepherd stretches her arm to point in the direction of the East, the extended arm of the angel holding the candle crosses with it.

ANGEL

Jesus your Savior is born!
Come and see Him!
Come and adore Him!

CHORUS

COME AND SEE HIM! COME AND ADORE HIM!

The Chorus now moves solemnly in procession from the side staircases to join the Shepherds on the middle staircase, singing along with the Congregation who are now asked to join in:

O come let us adore Him!
O come let us adore Him!
Christ the Lord!

Chorus of Sheep settle down on the main staircase around the Shepherds and the Holy Family, the Angel standing by.

A reading from Matthew followed, given by the narrator, where the Magi make their appearance to Herod. These wise men descended upon the scene in spendidly colorful procession from the sacristy from behind the altar. Appearing before Herod, who had in the meantime sprung up from his place at the bottom of the stairs, they addressed to him the words:

Wise Men
Where is He that is born King?
We saw a Star!

Herod, as we know, is troubled by these words and deceit-
fully asks them to return to let him know where this Child is
to be found, but the Magi are later diverted from this course
by the appearance of an angel in their dreams who warns
them not to return to Herod. The whole was read out at the
time by the narrator, before and after the Magi offered their
obeisance to the Child, which they did sumptuously, with all
the others sitting round the Holy Family on the main staircase
looking on in wonder, while Herod continued to stand tall
before the congregation in the foreground.

*

At the time, the drama I had helped put on (naive though this
was in form) became my own personal journey through the
Christian mysteries (one of many that I was to take over those
many years). It was to be repeated at the Christmas celebration of 1987, and it was followed at the Easter celebration in
the spring of 1988 by a drama about the Resurrection, which I
based entirely on pieces from the account out of St. John. The
actors spoke all of the drama, which is to say, there was no
narrator in this instance, and the interesting bits of stage
action included, first, the procession of the Resurrected Christ
from the back of the Church up the main aisle of the nave
while the main actor at the time, a girl who played Mary
Magdalene, stood facing the altar, ignorant of His approach,
though of course the congregation saw Him approaching.
The main interest of the stage action at this point centered on
Mary whom I had repeatedly "turn" to the Christ ("turning,"
as John intends, in a progressively more and more intense

vision of Him) when the Resurrected Christ first announces His Presence. I had her "gyrate" to her right to look down at Him as He stood first at the bottom of the staircase, and when He had ascended the stairs, going around her, I had her "gyrate" again to her right to look up at Him, as He now stood above her on one of the upper steps.

In the meantime I had Mary shed her dark brown cloak, which she wore as a symbol of the Earth's wintry death, to reveal prominent inter-crossing ribbons hanging from her blouse — one in spring green, the other in passion red symbolizing the redeeming blood of Christ. "I have seen the Lord," Mary tells the disciples, who had by now joined her at the bottom of the staircase, and, when the Christ addressed them with the words: "Peace be unto you," they too shed their cloaks to reveal the same combination of spring colors on their shirts. At the words: "Receive ye the Holy Ghost," the actor who played the Christ proceeded to give away the lilies he held in his arms through the medium of Mary whom I now had mounting the stairs to gather them from Him. Another nine disciples now joined the main two I had stationed at the bottom of the staircase, all of them in the same colors, while the lilies were now dispensed all around. In the end the actor who played Mary had one lily left over, besides the one she had kept for herself, and, thinking of what she might do with it, she finally decided, without prompting from me, to hand the lily back to the actor playing the Christ. Accomplished so spontaneously, the gesture had a sublime effect and seemed to put the perfect finishing touch to the enactment of this greatest of all dramas. A woman who had worked on the performance with me proceeded after this to a brief commentary to the congregation, among other things on reasons for the choice of colors for the performance, so that everything might be carefully appreciated.

This performance of the Resurrection-drama constituted a special addition to the power and mystery of my
experience of the Easter celebration that year, and the whole
compounded my Easter experience of the previous great
spring. They were to remain the two most powerful experiences of my life, in a general period of my life that was
certainly my life's great moment. I would help to put on yet
one more play that would see me through the whole sequence of the Christian mysteries, as if by way of summation.
This was for the parish-school celebration of the Assumption
of the Virgin Mary. The event that year had been selected as
a fitting moment to pay tribute to Joe for his twenty-five years
as a priest. It was being organized by one of the CND nuns
associated with the parish, who had long been associated
with the school as the Music teacher there. The drama I put
on I pieced together in this case from several of the Gospel
texts, ranging over the whole action from the time of the
Annunciation through the Passion and Death and Resurrection right up to the final Assumption of Mary. While Mary
and John stood beneath Christ on the Cross — at the words
that Christ speaks to Mary: "Woman, behold thy Son!" and to
John: "Behold thy mother!" — I had Mary dramatically hand
over a copy of the Bible, arms fully outstretched, to the actor
playing the Evangelist. The gesture was for the edification of
the many school children who were looking on from the
audience. The climactic moment came when the actor who
played the part of Christ (the same actor who had played
Herod in the Christmas play) spoke the lines that Christ
speaks at the moment of His Death: "It is finished!"

All who took part in the play had, up to that moment,
been holding lit candles, which were now all blown out together, until angels who stood behind the outstretched arms
of the crucified Christ, their own candles remaining un-
quenched, in the very moment that the Christ revives offered

to re-light the candles of all, once again through the first
agency of the actor playing Mary Magdalene. Also given was
the scene between Christ and Peter where Christ asks him
repeatedly: "Do you love me?" — until the final injunction
is given: "Feed my sheep . . ." The last words of the John
Gospel were also read: "And there are also many other things
which Jesus did, but the world itself could not contain all the
books that would be needed to tell us everything that Jesus
did." The presentation was then brought to a close with a
symbolic crowning of the Virgin Mary by John and the Angels
and a singing of the Immaculate Conception, in which all of
the audience were finally asked to join in. It was to be the
crowning in another sense of the whole of my recent experience while at Willibrord's.

*

Throughout the period from the spring of 1987 to the late
spring of 1988 I continued to pursue my in-depth reading of
Rudolf Steiner's Anthroposophy, which at that time I concentrated, appropriately, on his great Christological cycles of
lectures, beginning with the lectures on Luke, and continuing
with Matthew, Mark and John in that order. I conducted these
readings in my new quarters in that large room in Westmount
on Dorchester Street, which served as an ideal setting. For the
first time in my life I felt I had separated myself from preor-
dained social-cultural practices that insisted, for instance, that
one would have to live in a full-scale apartment, with all of
one's furniture around one etc. My powers of mind and spirit
thrived on the near-mystical freedom that suddenly came
with the dramatic unconventionality of living very simply in
a room that made a strong aesthetic impression with its high,
ornate ceilings and massive door, though the room was otherwise very simply furnished, mostly in white. A wooden

writing table, painted white, was set up against the very high window to the back of the house, which was overspread with a beige curtain patterned with golden brown and green leaves. From the window I had the view of a young, slender elm tree, among an entire line of elms that stretched themselves along the length of a quiet lane that ran perpendicular to the backyard. Beside the table in the far corner of the room was a white wicker reading chair, with royal-blue cushions. There was also a white-grey carpet in the center of the room on a wooden floor and a single bed in the corner covered over with a huge, overhanging counterpane also white and beige.

It was here that I would begin to put down my thoughts about what I considered to be the great line of criticism on Shakespeare since Swinburne — writing which would eventually form the opening section of the third chapter of my second book, though the article I intended at the time never did materialize. In the meantime I had had further success in getting a second article accepted, gleaned from other material on *Hamlet* edited from the thesis, which was to have the title: "Hamlet and the Fortunes of Sorrowful Imagination: The Genesis and Fate of the Ghost." This edited material was to re-appear as the first chapter of my first book. Staying on in my room in lower Westmount, I had remained in the neighborhood of Marilyn's apartment, though in the meantime she had moved out into the east end to be closer to the Hospital. Absorption in my spiritual-intellectual interests was once again slowly beginning to isolate me in my mind, though Marilyn and I continued to see each other almost every day. By late spring, though I could not justify the idea from any practical consideration, I had become obsessed with the idea of returning to England. Because of my fast dwindling finances, I felt it would be my last chance for some time of getting back there, before I would be forced to take up yet another middling job (for in the meantime my tenure at the

College had ended), though what this job would be I could not say.

In the end I did get over to England, where I was to stay for all of three weeks. Primarily I was to spend the greater part of my day at the British Museum Library to which I had direct access as a graduate doctor of a British University, and in these august surroundings I continued my slow work of research and writing on Shakespeare criticism. In other respects this was to be my farewell visit to England. I had made arrangements to see Nicholas who by then was living in London in his retirement in rather meagre fashion, bringing his long study of the baroque aspects of Shakespeare's art to consummation in his Oxford edition of *Macbeth*. To this very day I can remember him waving back to me at what I felt even then was our final farewell, when each of us turned round again to catch a last glimpse of the other after we had first parted. On this visit, I would roam the streets of London quite aimlessly, in a melancholy stupor, and I especially recall my awe-struck visits to Westminster Abbey and to St. Paul's, where I attended a Sunday service, and my walk along the whole length of the graceful Thames to get from one sacrosanct place to the other. I thought London simply the most beautiful city in the world and (in spite of its whirlwind pace, which merely inspired *me* to an idea of intense literary activity) in its grandeur the most humanly dignified and the most humanly comfortable city (at least in those parts that are dignified and comfortable; one simply has to have the experience of walking through downtown London on a Sunday or a holiday, when the streets are, oddly enough, very largely deserted). Most especially, I remember my visit to the National Gallery where I was to stand in a visonary daze before the most extraordinary painting I had ever seen — the early Crucifixion, by Raphael, painted when he was nineteen, from the Città di Castello Altarpiece.

For more than three hours I sat before this painting in a rapt contemplation in which my wonder grew and grew. Uncannily, I was looking upon the very same scene I had so prominently highlighted in the dramatic enactment I had just put on at the Willibrord's parish school. This scene I knew is the one that mattered most to Joe: the scene that matters most also to the Mother and to John, her new son, who stand beneath the Cross in the painting. I was then (as much as this seemed possible to me) standing before the Cross myself, as I had never stood before it in the past — the Light of the Resurrection seeming to stream out from that whole background landscape behind the Cross, as only Raphael could mediate that Light to us. No one who has not stood before the very painting can appreciate how uncannily powerful Raphael's representation of that Light is. Here too were the splendid colors that in my own poor way I had tried in the Easter play to show reflect the working of that Light out of Nature. I also knew by then what a central figure Raphael was in the account of our spiritual history that Anthroposophy offers, though I did not know it to the point I do today. I had felt the obsessive need to go to England, I knew even then, because I had been called to see, to stand and to sit or bow before this great painting of extraordinary mystery, which seemed to have been intended for me as a kind of revelation bringing together all the deepest strands of my recent "moment," stretching back to the time when I had first begun my apprenticeship at Willibrord's, and with Anthropo-Sophia as my young guide.

VI

On my return to Montreal, I would re-assume quarters this time in a very small room on the second floor of the house that belonged to my Hungarian family friends, who were always ready to accommodate me again. From that second-storey perch, from the kitchen area at the back door, I could now look down rather than up upon that tall slender elm tree that for me will always mark the spot in my memory. Roused by my recent trip to England, I began in these new quarters what was to be a new article on a theme I had been carrying about in my head for a long time, ever since I had first begun research on Shakespeare years earlier. It would turn out to be the article "Othello's 'Sacrifice' as Dialectic of Faith," to become later the first chapter of my second book. Especially I remember working out my ideas and reading Kierkegaard's *Fear and Trembling*, while sitting luxuriously under the sun with Marilyn under a large grove of elm trees to the north end of the pond at Angrignon Park. To this day I can still see Kierkegaard's book lying there momentarily abandoned in the tall grass, his face placidly looking out at us from the book's cover. That was when Marilyn and I had stopped to play scrabble, which was a favorite pastime of hers. I would recall this pastoral moment as among the very last that I would spend with Marilyn, in that "separate peace" that seemed to define us in our very essence.

Within a few months of my return to Montreal, I would agree to move into the old apartment on de Normanville that Ivana and Jasmin were now vacating. It seemed to us all at the time a question of a proper passing on of the heritage. The

move brought me strategically closer to Marilyn's place in the
east end, and the sense of wide open space that I had experienced while first in that apartment was now returning to me.
The world would indeed open up to me again but dramatically, far beyond what I could ever have expected or desired.
On November 2nd, 1988, my father passed away, after a short
and severe illness that he bore with great dignity. Among
other things over this time, I especially remember helping my
mother through the event with a prayer for the dead by
Steiner's own hand that I passed on to her. She took the
prayer up with fervor, in a complete confidence that I was
offering her all that was needed, and she repeats it on her
knees every night to this very day. It was a devastating experience for me as a member of my family to be now taking my
turn in one of those funeral cavalcades that we had always
seen passing by in the streets of the city over the years. There
we sat now ourselves in the official family car, to watch the
coffin that contained my father being carried down the
church stairs to the hearse in front of us and set into it. I
remember my sister, aghast with the pain of her loss, especially needing attention from me that day.

My father had been taken by death at the relatively early
age of sixty-seven, and it seemed to me that we had been
somehow injured by the death and humbled, as if the great
pride my father had always expressed in himself and especially in us, his own kind, had taken a beating and we were on
display to all the others, suddenly dispossessed. My father
had always been thought of as the leader of our large extended family, and we ourselves had been made special as his
own family on account of that status of pride he bore. His was
the first death in the family since his own father had died, and
there was not to be another death for years to come. It was in
that time that we also gave up our family country-place, for
my father, knowing that he was dying, had been intent on

ensuring that my mother would be well provided for. There could be no question of her staying on at the country-place to which they had retired, for the isolation would have been killing, and there were no savings for her, so that the place had had to be sold to make way for the kind of money that my mother would need to set up in a modest mobile-home just down the street from where my sister lived on the island of Laval. And so, with my father's death, there passed away also the place that represented the heart and the life-blood of my youthful imagination and my primal "link" back to the eternal from this world. My father had taken this "link" back with him into the otherworld . . . I had been "cut off" — in a far, far deeper sense than I could imagine.

In the meantime, Dvorak's *Symphony of the New World* was the piece with which I consoled myself and continued the journey with my father into his new life. My father's spirit would indeed remain with me for a good many years to come, and in no simple, vague sense only. I might even say, along a certain train of reasoning faith, that through his mediation, in death, I was spared a terrible injury and might even have been saved from death myself — for what was in fact a third time. Not long after my father's death, I was making my way to the graduate study library at Concordia from the Stanley Street entrance, when I stopped just inside the building's doors, distracted by the sight of an old man on the street, who was just about half bent-over in his walk, carrying his shopping bags with an utmost resignation and an admirable sufferance: the extent of his ailment, and the way he bore it, had entirely possessed me in that moment. I had forgotten where I was, had altogether lost consciousness of my purpose in being there, when the impulse came into my mind to move on. It was then that I felt an overpowering shadowing presence stretching itself well above my head and down to a point just about where my shoulder blades lie. I had been stopped from moving, suddenly realizing that my impulse to move would have had me turning down into a very steep staircase that yawned ominously at my feet. There was no doubt in my mind that in my own will I would have turned and fallen precipitously down those horrid stairs, a fall that might well have permanently injured if not killed me, whereas another being had in that moment stood watch over me and alerted me providentially out of *its* will.

I had thought this the work of an angel-being, had felt its presence as powerfully as one would sense the presence of one whom one knew to be actually there, until I came across an account in my reading of Steiner, somewhat uncannily as it turns out, not long after the event, which indicated that in the case of someone who has just died one's angel may be availed of by that soul to communicate warning about a threat to one's life. Apart from this episode, however, I must say that I have stayed close to my father only in my dreams, which have invariably taken the same form. When I have had these dreams, it has always been the case that I am holding on to him tightly, in an uncontainable grief of outpouring love and sworn devotion, and in great tears that never seem to end. It is just like one of those great dream-visions that one meets up with in so many places in English medieval literature. To my father I also owe indirectly another crucial encounter in my life, for it was at his death that my old friend, Luigi, brought along Antonio D'Alfonso, with whom I had lost contact over the years. "The death of a parent is a hard thing," he said to me on seeing me then, and it was on meeting me in that moment that Antonio proposed I send him a manuscript for publication. In the interval of eleven years since we had last seen each other, he had succeeded in building up a reputable publishing house, and he was keenly interested in having something from me. I slowly began to put together the text that would become *Otherworldly Hamlet*, my first book. Not for another year and a half, however, would the manuscript be ready for Antonio's further editing, though in this case little editing would be required of me.

*

Within two months of my father's death, in January of 1989, I was offered a full teaching workload at Concordia University, and so began a career as a university Lecturer that would last for ten years up to this day. In my second year of teaching, at McGill University, in a course I gave on Jacobean Drama, I would have the opportunity to work out further my thoughts about the influence of Martin Luther on Shakespeare and, through Shakespeare, on his Jacobean contemporaries. It had long been my view (ever since I had first come across Hiram Haydn's account of Martin Luther in what I regard as the greatest book on the period, *The Counter-Renaissance*) that Shakespeare, like Christopher Marlowe before him in his *Dr. Faustus*, was profoundly influenced by Martin Luther in writing *Hamlet*. It was extraordinary timing, since the further research I was able to do on Luther, while at McGill, would finally help to establish my reading of *Hamlet* in my book on firm grounds. And so was born the Preface to the book, which I would not pen until the spring of 1990, after my year of teaching at McGill. It was one of the few times that I remember Antonio commenting effusively on my work to say that he thought the piece especially good. At the same time, here I was bringing into published form a study of *Hamlet* that had concentrated from early on on the theme of death, the challenge of discovering a world beyond it and the boundaries it set to that special effort of imagination, and all this was now taking final shape around the death of my own father, whom I had, in the indirect way I have just described, credited for the prospect of my publishing the book at all. Inevitably, the book was dedicated to my father, the relevance of whose presence in death to the book's theme was not lost on one reviewer of the book later, whose own eye was open to this metadramatic dimension. In the meantime, in September of 1990, my piece on *Othello:* "Othello's "Sacrifice' as Dialectic of Faith', would come out in *English Language Notes*.

My reading of *Anthroposophy* continued strongly at this time and remained my main work of research over the period from 1985 onwards. I had covered much ground, having added especially in-depth studies of works such as *Knowledge of the Higher Worlds, Christianity as Mystical Fact* and *Occult Science,* and by the spring of 1989, I had finally become, through Eric's personal recommendation, a member of the Anthroposophical Society in Canada. I was in my obsessive "Orphic" mode again, separated from Marilyn for long periods of time by the onerous teaching load I would inherit very often at the last minute, so that sudden long preparations would be needed (especially in the novel and in preparing my lectures on Shakespeare). Otherwise I was separated from Marilyn by my reading of Steiner, which I would insist on doing whenever I found time away from my strenuous teaching duties. My relationship to Marilyn had become consequently somewhat strained, though our mutual devotion continued.

I remember two incidents that stand out with a special poignancy, both of these on the occasion of my birthday. In my first year at Concordia, Marilyn surprised me by showing up with a gift, after my class was done, in the Norris building, after a long period in which we had not seen each other. In the following year when I was at McGill, I would find her in the evening of that same day, waiting for me in her car, which was parked along the street where I lived, though she could not have known when I was to return from my office at McGill that evening and no doubt had been sitting there for hours. The sadness of my haunted life returns to me when I think that I did not and could not take the time to be with Marilyn then as I might have wished: if only I had not felt so pressed to accomplish all that I had set out to do, modest though all this seemed to be. Willibrord's remained another constant obsession, from the time it had opened up to me an experience of the great Christian Mysteries about which I was finding all the clarification I needed from Steiner's Anthroposophy. My longstanding confrontation with the theme of death — the way into it or through it, or the way out of it, on which my study of *Hamlet* had dwelt, continued as the primary motivation in my life. This theme was now being refracted out of the very pattern of my life in the direction I was taking with my literary work, though the pattern was as yet far from fully clear to me.

*

Yet the act of "reflection" on the pattern of my life had begun. It had begun as a series of "returns," the first of which had been my return to the de Normanville apartment. Here I would vigorously take up once again my intellectual role partially cast off during the years of what I might call my spiritual initiation. In July of 1990, I would choose to leave de Normanville once again for the neighborhood of Willibrord's, to take up residence on a street, for that cultural context of my life, appropriately named Joseph Street — no doubt because of the view of St. Joseph's Oratory that one had unobstructedly from the north end of that street. However, I did not have that view from my present apartment, as I did when I was last in Verdun, and that too seemed poetically appropriate for this time. Living at some distance from the parish while at my de Normanville address — so that I no longer got down to the church liturgies as often as in the past, I had begun to sense my growing distance from the parish life that had afforded me the experience of so many mysteries. I had the hope that by moving back I might be able to recover these mysteries, to live my way back into them as it were, though already I felt they were passing away from me in that particular form at least. The spiritual magic in that parish could still be found, but it had grown more incidental and was now less dramatically apparent, though the drama would again surface in a grand way on occasion.

Thus, I recall the long Easter Vigil celebration held in the spring of 1991 on Easter Saturday night (the Vigil serves in most parishes today for the Easter celebration itself). We were all still in the mood of the Crucifixion event, and there seemed to be so little life or light in us to speak of. Joe was struggling through his homily, as though he were desperately searching for his own way through the event, so that I remember sensing for a moment that he was not, and would not be, working his usual, legendary magic that night, for all was emptiness and darkness in the church still. But there suddenly followed a dramatic "breaking loose" that was altogether unexpected, since we had more or less accepted that nothing would be streaming forth that night, as Joe finally settled upon the portentous words he had seemed to be looking for all this time:

"And so, HE came to stamp OUT death!!

A great tone of victorious accomplishment suddenly rang through the church at that moment, so that the space of the church was filled with a light among us that was now chasing all darkness away, and we were transformed around that light, which was suddenly all of our own making, achieved in response to the powerful work Joe had once again accomplished in opening that space to us.

Joe's momentous spiritual powers seemed to be paving the way for a form of knowledge that continued to tantalize and elude me. He seemed possessed of fitful insights from a greater whole within himself that I never doubted he understood in the depths of his holy being, but it would be in some respects my own task to seek to find the basis for a clearer and more reliable way of knowing this greater whole, and it is to Anthroposophy that I was turning for more comprehensive elucidations. My reading of Anthroposophy was constant and occupied me for much of the time that I was not attending to my teaching duties at Concordia, but eventually a sense of my isolation set in again from the inconvenience of my physical location in Verdun. I had landed myself back into the very situation of intense loneliness that had plagued me for so long before I moved out of Verdun the first time into my room in the city. I sensed that I was also losing hold of what had brought Marilyn and me together; I was desperately trying to hang on to what was slipping away. In the circumstances, I decided that the best option would be to move back once again into the city where I might reclaim some of the original magic I once shared so intensely with Marilyn and still be in reasonable distance of Willibrord's which I would continue to visit. Thus I found myself in late August of 1991 once again "returning" this time to St. Marc Street, into an apartment that lay farther down the street though part of the same building in which Marilyn had had her apartment, on a third storey that had a balcony at the back and from which I could look down once again on that same overgrown backyard with that same powerful password — *Braziland* — painted over the far wall, also that same illustrious bedroom to that wall's far left that had once been a sacred ground. From this greatly satisfying perch I could see at the same time, over to the right, that stupendous cross that adorns the tall steeple of the Marguerite D'Youville center on St. Mathieu Street — the center that

has been run, for so many generations, by the devoted order
of the Grey Nuns on behalf of single mothers abandoned by
their society. My book on *Hamlet* had also recently been published (thirteen years later, work that I had written when I
was twenty-five — as far back as 1978!) And so, one might
think I had managed, by an artful scheme of some ingenuity,
to keep the several main elements of what had been the best
part of my former life together.

*

But once again the center would not hold. By the end of
September, Marilyn had settled on the idea of her holidaying
in Greece. This had been the great dream-idea we had enter-
tained between ourselves ever since we had first met and I
had shared with her my sense of her embodying, in the look
of her eyes, the divine beauty of that Graeco-Roman epoch
into which Christ had incarnated. But now she had decided
to go there on her own. We had been estranged over several
months, and she had felt the need to get away, especially from
the rigors of her demanding work. Oddly enough, while she
was away, I found myself listening to Mozart's *Così fan tutti*,
concentrating especially on the moment when the unfortu-
nate males conceive the idea of pretending to leave their
respective wives, on the view that they can thereby prove
their wives faithful when each male returns in disguise to woo
the other's wife. However, in the moment when the women
are saying goodbye to their men, Mozart's music insists that
we understand, all too sadly, that all are saying goodbye
forever to their innocence, since the ploy will prove the
women indeed assailable in love. Marilyn would return from
Greece with a remarkable blanket made in that region and
marked with special symbols which apparently represented
eternal life, and that blanket would continue to lie over my

bed for years to come as a memento of our deep time together,
but already on her return it was known to us both that our
relationship had come to an end.

I would go through this latest break-up with far less
distress than I had known in the past, largely because, while
a couple, Marilyn and I had spent a good deal of time apart,
not seeing each other for weeks at a time. The pathos of this
loss, for all that, is no less searingly registered in my soul. I was
coming to the end of my mystery "life," if I may call it that,
coming to the end of it in that immediate form at least, and I
would soon be "cut off" almost entirely, living in that break-
down of *all* belief, about which I would write later in my
second book — although I hardly knew what I was passing
through at the time. Certainly by August of 1993, from a note
I put down in my journal for that time, Willibrord's too would
soon be "over" — "over," that is, as a great spiritual-cultural
influence in my life, though I continued to attend the
Eucharistic Liturgy (by which, as a form of meditation on the
Christian mysteries, I have always been greatly impressed),
and I continued to offer my services as a reader on occasion,
well into 1994. In the meantime, my commitment to Anthroposophy continued unabated, and I was also being kept busy.

*

In January of 1992, I was to be offered part-time work as a
Lecturer at the Université Laval in Quebec City, to which I
would commute once a week. That was on top of the Lectur-
ing job I continued to hold at Concordia. Laval offered a basic
program of studies in English Literature, taught entirely in
English, to a modest number of Quebecois students who had
acquired a passion for that Literature. The program was otherwise kept burgeoning by the many other students who,

registered for the program in English as a Second Language, were also required to register into three basic Genre courses from the program in Literature: in drama, poetry, and short fiction. I found myself, for the first time since my youth, once again wonderfully immersed in the Quebecois culture to which over the years I had remained intellectually (if not politically) oblivious, though, as a Quebecois who spoke the language, I had always been, in another sense of course, steeped in the culture, living in it from day to day. My experience at Laval would be re-inforced later by yet another tenure held at the Université du Québec à Trois-Rivières, a tenure that would last for two years, from 1994-1996.

I was now being "asked" to bestow all that I had acquired in the way of training in English Literature upon my own Quebecois kind, and the results were uniquely satisfying. Teaching at university can be, for the most part, a thankless job, but at Laval I always felt uniformly thanked and very warmly at that, and there never were any personality problems from students (in the case of these problems, arrogant souls who always already know better or know it all before they undertake to learn anything new. When one is faced with these problems, one has no choice but to deal with them with a longsuffering patience that finally compromises teaching) — problems such as I had continually encountered both at Concordia and McGill.

This fresh period in my life, which would last for about two years, would be marked by my personal relationships with two young Quebecois women, both of whom were from the country. With one of these, Line (pronounced Lynn), a woman of thirty, I would have a relationship over most of that time. My time among this folk would be primarily one of poetic culture. Not that I pretended to penetrate Quebecois intellectual culture, for I never felt I knew the language well enough for that; nor could I even begin to make sense of the

regional differences that go to making so much of what Quebecois culture is all about, since I had never actually made
friends from that culture or really lived in it at all. However,
being Quebecois in blood always connected me directly to
these people when I spoke to them, whether in English or in
my lame French, and what I especially had by way of connection to them was a wonderfully poetic relationship to nature's
scene, which I am quite sure came alive to me in a quite
particular way in this period from the fact that I had penetrated their culture spiritually at some level.

There was in one instance a continuous series of "images," accompanying points of departure from and return to
my teaching in Quebec City — for my tenure at the university
there would be interrupted between the spring of 1994 and
the summer of 1995. In May of 1994 I was on my way out of
the city by bus, crossing the Pont Pierre Laporte with its
astounding view of the cliffy environs and powerful river that
mark Quebec City so distinctly from that vantage point. After
a long day spent dining and walking along that river, I had
just parted from Josianne, a young woman of twenty-three,
with whom I had had the friendliest relationship while there.
There had been some prospect of a closer relationship with
each other, though nothing was to transpire along these lines.
The profoundly social nature of Quebecois life, even among
lovers, would not really admit of my kind of solitary existence,
and that contrasting situation seemed to be reflected back to
me directly in the scene that saluted me from the river's
surface on my way out that spring.

On crossing the bridge at that point there were a good
many sailboats — as many as fifteen or perhaps twenty dot-
ting the river to my left as far as the eye could see, as the river
drove on towards Quebec City and the sea beyond, while on
the river to my right, in the direction of Montreal, to which I
was now returning, there was but the one sailboat lingering

in the shimmering of the water that was found only on that side since the sun was on that side. That very scene was to be mirrored back to me on this occasion with an uncanny congruency on my way into Montreal, on the still grander Jacques Cartier Bridge, though the view from there is not nearly so splendid. There next to the Old Port Tower to my left, the sight of whose picturesque simple structure always celebrated for me my entrance back into the city, on this perfectly clear day, once again there drifted on the same river that one sailboat and no other — drifting there, so it seemed to me, as the image of the solitary destiny to which I was returning. Strange to say, on my first re-entering Quebec City on my return in May of 95, I was greeted off the same bridge to my left by the same scene, with the single sailboat, as had bade me a dramatic farewell on my way out of the city the last time I had left it. With every new week that spring, as I entered the city to give class (it was to be my last term there), the scene on the river evolved, or rather changed, first from a solitary sailboat like the one of that former time, then to a steamship and sailboat without a sail, to steamship alone, to nothing in the end but the strong expanse of the driving river itself, which continued on its way to the sea ever implacable and undeterred in its ongoing course, to which there is no end.

*

It was also in this general period, while I was still associated with Laval, in July of 1993, that I made, rather fittingly, yet another "return"—to the setting of the river that I had known when I had last lived in Verdun with Pnina and the children. I would take up a large and the grandest apartment I had ever had, on La Salle Blvd, just up the street from where I had lived formerly, once again in spite of every instinct that said I was far better off in the city. This was a widely laid-out apartment with seven rooms, and with a long, well-built balcony at the front, from which one could look over, with even greater vantage, the grand old river scene that I had formerly made my own. This was a time of renewed loneliness in spite of my teaching routine and continued connection to Willibrord's as well as an ongoing love-affair with Line, with whom I had fallen in love on an outing in the Old Port and with whom especially I associated the old Tower. Line's profound family ties among five brothers and sister, as well as to her own family countrystead to which she remained attached in a primal way, had necessarily made a partial affair of our relationship and had put an end to my dream of a family with her. Nevertheless I would remain forever grateful to her for her continuing friendship over this time, which lent crucial support to me in my loneliness and allowed me to write again successfully.

Nature's scene in this period of my life continued to reflect the most marvellous "images" to me in so many astounding ways, all of which related directly to my lonely condition. My journal records numberless episodes of note, among which I find especially significant two that reflect on the limits of passion between the sexes. I had gone down to the river one early afternoon, with the sight of the peaceful current before me and the shimmering of the sun on the water, when a strange couple entered the picture to sit on the park bench right before me. I was sitting on the grass. The woman was very young and very dark and very beautiful, but she was in the arms of a much older man who was not beautiful and who might indeed have been her father. How a young woman so beautiful could be attached to "that," as I put it to myself at the time, I could not know, but it spoke of the tyranny of sexual needs, which I sensed also from the other side, for how could that man have resisted being attracted to and wanting a woman like her if given such a chance? The image spoiled the mystical beauty of nature's scene that lay before me. A gull was standing close by me in the grass looking out on them also, and it seemed astonished as well, astonished and profoundly annoyed, and even the wind ordinarily ruffling up the back of this gull seemed, by comparison, to bestow a mystical dignity on the bird. In another instance, the moon was settling just before nightfall above the magnificent poplar trees that line the river's edge in that same spot, bringing out the mystery in people's faces, when a well-dressed girl, in white pants, stopped in front of one of the lamp-posts that also line the river's edge, insisting on keeping her beau there, kissing quite passionately quite out of place in everyone's view while people were at all kinds of other things, and then a desolate young man came along who could not go by that scene without turning to look back at these lovers continually, for as long as they remained in his sight, as he found his way forward without eyes.

For the most part, however, the poetic "images" that came into view for me at this time spoke of something far deeper and purer than sexual relationships. Thus I record the sight, one early evening in late summer, of two blond children, very young, maybe five and two, sitting on opposite sides of their aging grandmother on a park bench by the river, the moon hanging over them massively, silver and white. Later, when it got dark, a frenetic black dog went by, by that time so much of a piece, in its wild effusive energy, with the moon that had grown more mysterious with a mist collecting. Or that very young abstracted boy, muttering to himself in play, with questioning brown eyes, standing just behind one of the lamp-posts by the river, when the day was still bright. Other images conveyed the mystical beauty of a perfect individual relationship to nature, as in the case of a young woman with tawny brown hair, dressed in grey and rose, whom I once saw by the river sprinkling bird-grain all about her, after which she set herself down to recline on the grass: birds gathered — gulls from every direction — virtually shrouding her: they swooped down around her in the softest blanket of forms of white and grey. I note further the image of a dog's tail, fluffy white and held high as it made its proud way along the river, which was itself bounded there by a seemingly endless line of poplars and *their* long white trunks: an apple tree in blossom stood in the foreground of my view.

From a human scene farther removed from nature's own landscape, I record other "images" that extend to periods of loneliness both from beyond the time of my return to the river and back in time before I made that return. I note especially on the bus one day that gorgeous young girl with both shins very badly bruised from a severe scraping up the whole of their length, also that lovely middle-aged woman, with her hair tied up, so elegantly dressed, with a crippled leg. I note too that young boy with scabs all around his mouth, with reddish, overgrown, disshevelled hair and badly torn pants: in spite of the wear and tear, he made every effort to tidy himself up, after he had gotten onto the bus, pulling the bottom of his very dirty trousers over his shoes. However lonely one may feel, one is kept intact from noting these "images" through which the Father continues to speak, calling our attention to a whole other world beyond ourselves. I note also that tall young boy, all bones and nothing else, skipping along the subway platform ahead of his grandmother. How naturally and lovingly she turns her attention to him, although he looks embarrassingly pathetic: he is joyful and excited from her loving attention nevertheless. On the way out of the station an elderly lady lies stretched out helplessly at the foot of a staircase, holding her ankle in pain, and a station attendant is seeing to her. He leaves her to call an ambulance, and I am struck by how nonchalant he is, walking to his purpose at a very ordinary pace, while in the interval a subway singer continues to sing unaware: "Are you warm? Are you real, Mona Lisa?" Yet nature's spirit could still hover over our alien modern scene, as in the further case I record of a young man with dog on a leash in the city, walking on with a greatly over-determined stride, and a helicopter flying in the vicinity — unbeknownst to the man, a stork flies by overhead, as if in blessing, as I watch.

I continued to be offered glimpses of the grace-filled days I had once known as a daily occurrence and record, in May of 1992, Mother's Day at Willibrord's, a visit to Rebecca, Terry's mother, also the visit I had with Joe on Marilyn's birthday three days before leaving Joseph Street in Verdun, to take up residence again on St. Marc, in 1991. As late as June 1994, when I was still in residence on La Salle by the river, I note an old lady with shopping bag where Verdun Street crosses Willibrord Street, also an old man with hunched back, standing separately from each other as both await the traffic light. Each life, though separate, is splendidly affirmed on this beautiful day that is being shared by all — as beautiful and wonderful to them, in their old age, as it is to the young. Or again, not long after I moved back to St. Marc in 1991, on my way to Luigi's for a visit, on another splendid day I note in a suburban backyard as I pass by, a young girl dressed in white, with black hair, her dog, also black, tied on a leash to the house and lying under the table at which she reads, a canary in a cage on top of the table chirping away. And the most remarkable perhaps of all these variegated "images" of the human scene: that of the "angel-boy" of perhaps six or seven, with curly blond hair, dressed in a dark-blue shirt and dark-blue shorts. He sits on a stone wall that goes round one of the many red flower displays that are to be found carefully arranged in that large square every spring and summer, just outside the Place D'Armes subway station on the border with Chinatown. The boy is twisted inwards towards the red flowers (a slender tree with its broad leaves hangs over him as if it might be hiding him), as he quietly twirls in one hand the long feather of a bird to which he seems to be communicating all of his many thoughts. He sits alone, in (what, it is clear, he supposes is) a perfect isolation, unvisited and unseen.

*

In what was to be my very last stay by the river, in the late spring of 1994, I would finally bring to a head the two main currents of my work undertaken over all these years: namely, Shakespeare and Anthroposophy, which I now found myself linking together. I would finally return, in the second of only two intervals of writing since I first addressed the subject back in 1987, to the material I had been painfully collecting for my second book, *Othello's Sacrifice*, to continue with the work of analysis I had begun on the history of Shakespeare criticism. This I would now link to the history of the Romantic Move-ment, which I was to argue culminates in the work of Rudolf Steiner. My creative effort in this moment was, in a certain sense, the culmination also of my life-struggle up to that point. I had come to the conclusion that the essential subject matter of Shakespeare's great tragic period lay, in the end, in his representation of the spectacle of the violent death of a loved one, and I had seen in my treatment of this subject matter at the same time a possibility for purging *myself* of the tragic guilt I carried from the many separations I had been through and the many "deaths" I had finally brought on, both in myself and in others. Through my treatment of this great theme in Shakespeare, I could now speak of the hope that awaited anyone who had been through tragedy of any kind from any form of tragic conflict in any part of the world, and so, out of a life that had not been lived politically, I seemed to offer hope in the deepest political sense. The way out of tragedy, I argued, was certain, based on a set of verifiable psychological laws that ensured our human evolution out of it. My triumphant "moment," if I might call it that, this period was otherwise marked by a loneliness that continued strongly and from which I found partial relief only in the Eucharistic liturgy I attended every Tuesday in the morning at Willibrord's, and I am altogether convinced that never would I have accomplished my work in the end without this support. Indeed throughout this latest period of my writing, the impression I had was of working continually *with* someone — the angel, my own or so I believe, with whose approval and through whose inspiration it was that I argued an elaborate case that seemed at the time to write itself.

VII

My move, in July of 1994, back into the city on Baile Street was marked by my feeling that I had finally justified what had felt like a lifetime's struggle (it was a period that had lasted fifteen years). I had taken myself back into the close vicinity of Marguerite D'Youville and record from my journal for this time the further "image" of a crow perched atop the magnificent gold cross that adorns the steeple of that center — a perfect symbol of the sense of triumph I experienced at this time. This cross grows only the more luminous in the dusk and in the darkness of night, and it is the most beautiful cross of any in the city, as I believe, by virtue of the unique moment it records of the vision once given to Marguerite D'Youville herself. My move into the city at this time coincided with my experience of the most sublime of all "images" given to me: in the large grass square just outside the Centre D'Architecture down Baile Street. It involved three young girls, all under twelve, circulating around an owner with two dogs one white the other black, in their movement among themselves falling into innumerable and endless combinations of pictorial beauty and grandeur. At one point, one of the girls ran away down the whole length of the grass square, carrying the smaller white dog in her arms as if it might be some lost sheep she had joyfully recovered. A shaft of light framed her for a brief second, cast through the surrounding buildings by the setting sun: of a fading rose color, it suddenly caught the girl as she ran by, radiating from the red band she wore, as well as from her dress which was designed with flowers, red and pink below her waist.

I was now back in the city alone and would continue to be plagued by loneliness, but I was possessed of a now near-perfect understanding of the main patterns of my life, at least from the time Judit had come into it to alter everything. I knew now that the Eurydice for which I had been reserved and preserved through so many relationships, was Anthroposophy, or rather the being who inspires the world-vision Anthroposophy mediates: namely, *Anthropo-Sophia* herself, though a fuller understanding of who this Being is would come only over the next few years of study.

Already I had been kept from pursuing the normal academic career for which I seemed designed by that fateful trip down to Oxford back in 1976 and the mysterious depression that ensued in me from that moment. I would be taken through a rather different course of training, of wider intellectual-artistic scope, that would bring me back into connection with Antonio D'Alfonso for one thing and into a freer *literary* mode of progress. The deeper spiritual influences that would affect the course of my life seemed to be already present in the period that was marked by the appearance of the three women at the grotto, as well as the Lazarus-episode represented on Ghiberti's doors that had absorbed me so intensely. Both episodes seemed to forecast the religious initiation I would undergo while at Willibrord's. Everywhere I seemed primarily taken with the religious element in sculpture and in painting, though this affinity for things religious seemed to affect me only subconsciously. The course of my life, it seems, would have to take me through my experience at Willibrord's *before* I could continue to pursue my academic career. It was a course of life that would set me back and keep me from becoming a full-time university professor with the usual academic destination. Years earlier I had made the choice of continuing with my own self-training, which seemed to offer a fuller and richer course of literary life, rather than submit to what I saw as the repressive practices of graduate training, when I had decided to withdraw from The University of Toronto and return to my writing on *Hamlet*. That choice, now that I think back, I had already made once before when I was given the option, on graduating from Loyola in 1974, of going to Yale, at which point I chose England, where graduate work is primarily self-directed.

My time with Ivana would bring to fulfilment a whole sentient experience that included Italian art and the mountains both of England and of Italy, as well as my long critical-intellectual training that included an intense exposure to music. Judit would then come into my life to deflect me towards an entirely unexpected encounter with Central Europe. Through this encounter Anthroposophy was circuitously making its way to me, for it is on account of the despair I went through over Judit that I turned with more eagerness than I would have, in the normal course of things, to Pnina at the time of her own appearance. An additional, gratuitous influence seemed always necessary to direct me into the deeper stream of life for which I had been chosen. Thus only after I had left Pnina, and had suffered from her insinuations that I was not made for it, would I begin to commit myself to Anthroposophy. Indeed, without the interest Pnina first took in Anthroposophy, the stage might never have been set for my own connection to it. Even so it would finally take the influence of Pnina's deliberate choice of fresh husband, Tibor Kalmar, to bring me fully round to the reality of Anthroposophy and its unmistakable relevance for my deepening experience of the world.

Still deeper influences seemed to have asserted themselves in the direction my life had taken, from what Anthroposophy confirms. For there we learn that before a child is born, the spirit-soul of that incarnation itself chooses what parents will offer it the bodily basis in life it requires to accomplish the purposes it has set for itself. Paloma had chosen me and her mother and would have necessarily sought to bring us together out of the spirit-world in order that she might have all that she needed for her own evolution as a spirit-soul. If that is the case, then I would have to attribute to Paloma, in her pre-birth existence, the role of prime mover behind the direction in Anthroposophy that was to characterize all three of our lives. Paloma, unlike Jasmin, would, until she turned twelve, receive the Waldorf education that is based on the principles of Rudolf Steiner's Anthroposophy. Paloma seemed especially meant for such an education, and one might think she might never have received it without the complex and painful configuration of events that dramatically brought Anthroposophy into her life through her mother's link to me. Underlying these connections, more mysteriously, had been my relationship to Eric who throughout the years had played the role of chief spiritual confidant in my life, as if he might be my remote Master directing the whole. Hence, I cannot forget, in seeking to understand this extraordinary concatenation of events, that it is I who initially chose Eric as my friend, years before Pnina would come into our lives. Perhaps already at that time I had some unconscious knowledge of all that would have to be. At the same time, Eric had, since his last visit to me in Verdun in the fall of 1990, strangely enough, fallen out of my life altogether — a further development that would allow me to evolve in an understanding of Anthroposophy on my own.

My life had constituted, at the same time, a meeting with many different peoples (quite apart from the many others I would meet as a language teacher — from East Asia, Latin America and the Persian Gulf most notably) from the Irish and Quebecois elements into which I had been born, and the American-Indian element, to further meetings through my sexual relationships, with the Italian, Russian and Jewish peoples, as well as, later, my own treasured Quebecois people. I would bear a special relationship of destiny also to the peoples of central Europe — those from Hungary (Eric being also of Hungarian ancestry), Romania, and later, in a member of the Society, the former Yugoslavia. I note as well the strong Irish-Scottish religious influence in my life, especially at Willibrord's, though I would count Marilyn's own kind of Jewish influence, in a rather more special sense, as no less religious. I seem in the pattern of my meetings with many different peoples to have been paving a path of universal experience, to be taken up literally by Paloma (who might be my Miranda), for in her life-blood and in the further pattern of her own relationships she seemed, via my difficult destiny, to be bringing the *whole world* together: and so, from my side the American-Indian element, from her mother's side the (Slavic) Russian and the Romanian, as well as the European Jewish, elements, and from my side as well the Irish element and the Quebecois element, while Paloma's relationship with her half-sisters assured her a continual contact with the more Mediteranean, Latin element in Jasmin who was Italian from her mother's side, and the Mediteranean African element in her other half-sisters from their father's side. Paloma seemed indeed to have been intended as an ambassador for the world in some sort — the very tragedy of my own life seeming from one point of view to pave the way for her — and I continue to have great hopes that she will play an important role in the world before long. As for Jasmin, she strikes me in my fancy as an old soul who seems to have been through it all before and is just remotely and patiently waiting for the rest of us to catch up.

*

I would spend the first period of my time on Baile Street vigorously typing up the manuscript of *Othello's Sacrifice*; among other things, I had deliberately set myself that work to offset the loneliness that continued. By the end of the summer I had done typing and would send the manuscript off to my publisher. The book would not come out for another two years — not until November of 1996 — after some lengthy discussions back and forth with Antonio about the many revisions that would be necessary. Unlike in the case of the first book, this one called for extensive re-writing of parts, and it was a singular experience, not to be forgotten, to work with an editor who knows what to insist on himself and what to acknowledge as right from his author, though the greater part of the revision I undertook involved re-organizing of my own fresh invention, pursued out of a general response to Antonio's acute, scrutinizing intervention into my work at this time.

In spite of the "triumph" I might claim for myself from one point of view, the work I had accomplished up to that point still seemed to me sadly limited. To some extent the books I had written certainly did reflect the range of intellectual progress I had covered and both the scope and the depth of experience I had passed through over the foregoing twenty years, and I could boast of some success in the reception of my first book, *Otherworldy Hamlet*, which had already been well noticed in major journals. What's more, I would ensure that the book would be fully noticed world-wide through the agency of the *World Shakespeare Bibliography*, which records all of these reviews and citations from year to year. In this manner I was ensuring the justification of my scholarly-artistic struggle, and over the following five years, more success was to come with *Othello's Sacrifice*.

But success of this sort could not satsify me. For one thing, I could not feel that these small books, though concentrated in their achievement and serving in intention to unify our view of Shakespeare, could even begin to do justice to the extent of the life-struggle that had surrounded their writing. I felt there had been far more to the life I had lived than what the books themselves could reflect, and for this reason I conceived of presenting the memoir that I am writing at this moment. Yet even now as I write, a huge gap interposes itself, a chasm that remains unjustified and unaccounted for, for it has always seemed to me that so much more might have come within the purview of my spiritual vision and the grasp of my critical representations in writing, so much more also by way of a further social function for myself in these terms, though to this day this function continues to elude me. I had made the death of the father my theme from *Hamlet* long before it interwove itself uncannily into my own life in the death of my own father, and "death of fathers," a major theme in *Hamlet*, I now came to see (with Shakespeare) as the main theme of our evolution out of the past. I continued with this theme in *Othello's Sacrifice* where it re-appears as the ultimate failure of the whole tradition of male heroism. It is the mother, I realized, who in her most honoured role now held the key to our evolution into the future, and the death of the mother (a transformation of the death of the loved one) would be the main theme of that further evolution. I had already touched on this theme in *Sacrifice*, while tracing the progress Shakespeare himself makes in these terms in his last plays. However, I would not be in a position to expound more directly on my new theme until I turned, three years later, to the writing of my next piece in this line of thought, in the summer of 1997: an essay to which I would give the title "Prospero's Powers," in which I focus on the mysterious sacrificial death of Prospero's wife through whom his own consummate powers come into being.

*

In the meantime I continued to pursue, beginning from that summer of 1994, a deeper philosophical inquiry into the basis of the Imagination as our chief vehicle of exploration into these matters. I sought to establish myself more fully in the theoretical account of our reasoning powers that Steiner offers by way of explaining *how* the Imagination emerges and develops — study that would require for the time being more extensive reading of Goethe, of Emerson and of the German Idealist Philosophers. I would have to find a way of linking Steiner and Goethe to English tradition via Coleridge and Emerson, beyond what I had already suggested about this link-up in *Sacrifice*, where I draw on Barfield's argument on behalf of the the link. While I began to immerse myself in this difficult new venture, the summer would bring in fresh distraction from my loneliness, and it is indeed curious how events concatenate. I had met a seventy-year-old man, of remarkable haleness and strength, at the Guy Favreau YMCA where I had been working out for a few years, and we had acquired the habit every so often of going for lunch after our work-out. Uncannily, his name was Kornel, which in German translates as "Crow"; he was a retired engineer, and we were planning an outing one day to a local brasserie of some note, when we discovered it oddly closed for the day. We ventured out subsequently into Chinatown, and I decided on a restaurant with buffet that I had been to a number of times in the past, though not often, and it is there that I came upon Wenjie who was serving our table.

I was more than struck by the great address and the great charm she displayed, which clearly showed her education. I had needed to use a telephone, but it turned out to be busy. Wenjie came over to the table some few minutes later to inform me that the telephone was now free, and as she said this, I could not help remarking on how stately she appeared in her manner. Attention of this sort is not what one would expect of someone serving in an ordinary Chinese restaurant. It was Kornel who insisted I pursue the matter with her; I recall his concern, after two weeks had passed, that I had not followed up on that first encounter. I *would* return, and, oddly enough, I simply went up to Wenjie, while she was having conversation with customers at one of her tables, and asked her out. She seemed quite pleased, in spite of the fact that she could barely remember having served me and did not really remember who I was.

I went out with her for the first time the evening of July 4 (American Independence Day), and I was astonished by the great artistic delicacy of her limbs (her arms especially), as well as by her lovely affection and friendly charm, and her tall gracefulness so youthful and so decidedly Oriental. She was a University graduate from Shenjhen University who had decided to make a new life in Canada. She thought there would be more promise for her here than in Hong Kong where she had worked for three years. I could tell that she had been one of the very best students at university simply from the intellectual pride with which she carried herself and the signs of excellence she sought in everything that surrounded her. Especially I remember, after I would accompany her the long route back to her sister's apartment in the West end, usually late at night, that final moment during which I saw her through her apartment building doors as I watched vigilantly from a distance. This was just the sort of behavior that an Oriental girl like herself would find most winsome, and for me today this ceremonious ritual of such simple innocence retains all the marks of an image that only sets off the irrecoverable past the more poignantly in my mind.

After merely a few months of taking her out after this fashion, Wenjie was now living with me. She had returned to her studies in Economics at McGill University and had two years left to complete on her degree. I would eventually meet her mother who had come over from the Republic of China to visit and was staying with Wenjie's sister. Both parents had been not-so-typical Communists over many years, and I was struck by the mother's perfect way of listening to what another person had to say before she would venture to speak her own mind, which she did in every instance without seeking to force her opinion in any way on her interlocutor. Of course I noticed this in the conversation this woman had with her daughters, with whom she was not always in agreement over their modern manners. Her own manners and behaviour showed a kind of training in dialectical exchange that I could see was based in that country's great Buddhist past which had carried over into the Communist present. Wenjie's upbringing had left her free to pursue her own life wherever that might take her, in spite of all differences her mother might express, which in any case centered entirely on what she saw as a failure of manners, ironically, in her already very refined daughters.

In December of 1994, I was married to Wenjie, in a Unitarian ceremony that would bring together my mother and elder brother from my own side and Wenjie's mother and elder sister and husband from her side. The ceremony took place in a makeshift chapel at the back of the Unitarian Church on Sherbrooke and McTavish. The church had burned down about seven years earlier when, in her enthusiasm for God, a frenzied organist took it into her head to set fire to the place. On the night the church burned down I was with Marilyn in her apartment on St. Marc Street; each of us had noticed separately how the apartment had suddenly filled with a gloomy, distressful darkness, and I remember speculating, after Marilyn and I learned of what had happened, that you would think whatever spirits the church had housed until then had sought shelter wherever they could and had settled on the apartment as one momentary abode. How strange to think that seven years later I would be married in the ruins of that church to Wenjie.

I saw in the marriage a prospect of settling down to an emotionally secure way of life; it had been Wenjie's dream to be married one day to a Westerner (as the Chinese call us), and there had been a strong romance on both sides. There was in any case such a disarming charm about Wenjie such as made one feel that with her one was recovering a second innocence, and the thought of her being rebuffed in any way by the hard reality in the West gave me the overwhelming urge to defend her. Wenjie had become a landed immigrant within a month of our first meeting, but I am quite certain that if she had not already achieved success in that venture, I should have offered to marry her anyway, even before the romance settled in and whisked us on with its own intrinsic force. Since Wenjie had much studying to do as an Economics student, I was left with much time on my hands for my work in Anthroposophy, once all my teaching duties had been seen to. I was to make great advances in my work at this time from the freedom of working in relative peace and security. However, the strenuous work schedules we had given ourselves to slowly wore away at the romance between us, and very soon we were no longer having sexual relations. This was to remain the main problem between us, though we were otherwise poignantly involved with each other emotionally, partly just from the fact that we were living together, partly because we were married to each other.

The loneliness of an unfulfilled marriage had in this way come upon me. Wenjie had always had the personality for getting out about town and seeing all she could while she was in Hong Kong, as well as in her social life before she met me. However, the prospect of working hard at her studies, which our life together had offered her, had now claimed her almost entirely and repressed what tendencies she might have had to indulge herself in the old way. She had become exceedingly good at school and was determined to be among the best graduating students. She refused to think there was any point in doing what I had always enjoyed doing in a small way, which was going out to sit and drink at a cafe, so that I found myself doing that alone, though I did not do this so very often. I had made a point of frequenting a small Italian restaurant called the Pastatell, to which I would go after swimming at the downtown YMCA — in a quiet, discreet setting on Stanley Street north of de Maisonneuve. Here I sat out on the street in relative peace although in the heart of the city, trying various kinds of port wine, which I had discovered for the first time. I sat there and dreamed of a life I might have been living somewhere in the region of Portugal where port was made and could be had cheaply, and not far from the seacoast which I thought must be astounding in Portugal. Here I might earn a living by teaching English to the local inhabitants and otherwise live only for what writing and thinking on the world I could still do. In the spring of 1995, Wenjie and I decided to move into another district closer to the McGill campus, on Milton Street between Park Avenue and Jeanne Mance. I found myself going for lunch after my swim to another spot altogether, a Lebanese eaterie, where I made the acquaintance, among those who served us, of a young Moroccan woman from Casablanca. It was clear that she was an educated woman, and, as it turned out, she had graduated with a degree in Architecture. She had followed her husband to Canada, but he had abandoned her not long after they had arrived, to go to California. It was clear that the events had left her heartbroken and disillusioned with men. Not long after I met her, she went down to California herself to settle divorce proceedings with her husband, and she would leave the eaterie almost as soon as she had returned. Some few months later I found myself, in a desperate loneliness of my own, going to the Alexandre Pub on Peel Street for early supper and discovered her serving there, quite by accident. She came up to serve me. She was in the same state of mind I had known her in, her own great melancholy in this moment responding directly to mine (tears even came to her eyes) while she stood over me exchanging casual news, till she had to go away to serve some others.

Her name was Raschida, a name glamorous enough to me on account of what I had read about Haroun-al-Raschid, the great Muslim Emperor of the eighth century who had developed the greatest civilization in the world at that time. His own name had been variously interpreted to me as Man of Wisdom and Man of Many Wives (had I not been a man of many wives?), and Raschida's own name now came across to me as Woman of Wisdom, Woman of Many Husbands. She was not a beautiful woman, but she had, as many Arab women do, the most beautifully shaped hands, and she had the very warmest heart.

The day had clearly brought us together, but she appeared to feign indifference of a sort, for she did not come back to my table when she could have, preferring to remain at the bar accommodating the chat there. Yet when we did exchange glances now and again, our hearts and affections spoke respectfully of each other. She seemed to be in despair of relationships, still nursing her broken heart, and she struck me as someone I had known for many years — like a wife of old, or at least each seemed to reflect to the other the state of being married. She seemed to stand before me as a symbol reflecting back to me the inverse pattern of my own life, according to which I had never been meant to stand by one woman or one wife. In that guise she looked out upon me not in judgment but with an unwillingness to think that she could ever devote herself again to a man, though it would seem she continued to wish that all might have been otherwise. When I left the Alexandre, I made sure I said I'd be back before she left for Morocco in the winter (for she had plans to return, now that her divorce was settled), but I never did go back, and I never would see her again.

*

While the study life on which Wenjie was bent did not allow us much diversionary life, it did have the effect of allowing me much time for my studies in Anthroposophy. It was the first time I could pursue these studies without any cultural contradiction in my personal life that tabooed such studies or resentment about my taking time over these studies, both of which checks I had been accustomed to getting from Marilyn and from Line. These studies I pursued in my own room in the apartment, which in my memory today has all the value and power of a great study-chamber where the bust of Hypnos continued to preside over my work, as it had for so many, many years. Here I had latterly put up Raphael's self-portrait, as well as a painting of Novalis, next to my reading chair, for my own inspiration and as a tribute to one of the great Individualities of the Anthroposophical Movement. I was studying about him in depth at the time. Here I brought my studies in Anthroposophy to a highpoint that I took the time to record in my journal: "Have now caught up with myself," my journal records, and "have covered the ground that I wanted to cover." I had now succeeded in researching the full range of Steiner's life-achievement, at least in respect of the main developments from beginning to end, as well as beyond, in respect of the responsibility Anthroposophists now bear towards the achievement Steiner left us, in the work of the Society itself. Significantly, I had recorded my own work-achievement into my journal (though I only now awaken to this, do not recall taking note of it at the time) on the day of Eric's birthday, August 15.

Ironically I had spent most of the many years since I had become a member of the Society mostly on my own. I had from the time Anthroposophy came into my life, and especially from the time Tibor had won me over to it, gradually gotten to meet most of the key personalities who were Members of the Society in Montreal, and for a time I had attended a study group with Eric, and I had also attended lectures in Montreal given by key personalities from around the world. However, there had been something about the study group that had alienated me from the first, a lack of what I would call essential seriousness. The approach to studying Steiner was either too casual, something to be had in own's own time and at one's ease as it were (one got up from the discussion-session to joke and laugh about as one would in any social group in any other sphere of life), or else the approach seemed to me ponderous in ways that imposed the unsubtle egoism of dominant personalities rather than any essential seriousness in the subject itself. I had stopped going early on, had subsequently become estranged from Eric in my decision no longer to attend. In this later period on Milton Street, however, I had judged myself ready — out of a hard-earned confidence of what Anthroposophy and the Movement are all about — to resume contacts, in order to take up a role of my own in the context of the Movement. My great hope was that out of my own now fully-informed and fully-developed inspiration I might find fresh meaning in the Society's continuing work, in spite of all the feelings I had had about it before. I was to be greatly disappointed, however, when I fell upon a more or less deliberate reluctance to have me back into the fold. I had resumed contact with Eric and had placed my confidence in him again, had asked him to let me know of any significant events that might be transpiring over the course of the upcoming year (all events at this time were received by word of mouth and were known only to a few), had received what I thought had been a heart-felt promise from him to do so, but I never did hear from him again, in spite of the fact that some major events did take place, as I learned later.

I was thrust back upon a deeper isolation than I had ever known before, spurned, and appalled by the egoistic politics that had determined Eric's refusal to open the doors to me, to which he would have no right by any standard of anthroposophical principles. I had been virtually excluded and recall my great resentment about Eric and those with whom I felt he monopolized Society activities, most of whom were of the Quebecois fold. Politics I had learned reigned here too. Beyond the book I had written, which had brought Shakespeare and Steiner into a dramatic relationship before the world, I would have no other outlet for the time being in the way of a continued expression in Anthroposophy, save what I would have to venture on my own. The burden that I felt in my isolation was more than I could bear, and for the first time I conceived a despair that I experienced as final — "a rage to end all things/To end what my laborious life imagined," as Yeats himself would have put it. My very life-struggle, which had involved giving up so much for so long from my unswerving commitment to Anthroposophy, had spectacularly come to nothing in social terms, had turned to outright mockery. Significantly, in light of the pattern my life had taken, it was my anthroposophical daughter, Paloma, who in this dire time would come to my rescue. She did so in a way beyond what I am sure anyone might have imagined, had the best scriptwriter in the world been offered the script to write.

Paloma had continued her visits to me, though she had interrupted them for a while, and it was on returning after a significant hiatus that she brought intense consolation in my distress. Not that she knew anything of what I was feeling about the Society, for I did not share these things with her, but without knowing it she did bring consolation nevertheless. She had slept over for the night in the bed that I used to sleep in on occasion. Early the next morning I had seen her off to school and the following night found myself sleeping in that same bed she had slept in. That night I had the most extraordinary dream I have ever dreamt. In my dream Steiner himself appeared to me, moving powerfully towards me from my left out of a corridor as I lay in a room — the mirror-image I now realize of my situation in the apartment, where the corridor was to my right. He came towards me with the powerful remonstration: "What else is there for us to do?", as if to say, "We must continue to work, whatever the circumstances that oppose us and though everything should range itself against us, for there *is* no other work of redemption." His image seemed to me to have joined with that of Joe Cameron, and it expressed anger with me over my despair. I remember waking up in the middle of the night from the sheer power of the dream, which had utterly unnerved me with its energy, filled as I was with terror of this presence, so overwhelming to my spirit. Yet I only wished to remain united with the power of this spirit that had appeared to me, as I lay in a wakeful terror; I only wished to prolong the effect of its visitation, in spite of the judgment and the anger that was being addressed at me. At the same time, I was quite certain on waking from this dream — my perception came to me instantaneously, along with the dream itself — that I had been able to have the dream only because I had gone to sleep in the very life-space (Anthroposophy calls it the etheric space) that Paloma had left behind her in that same bed from her sleep the night before — she who was herself the creation of Anthroposophy lived out at home and at school from day to day. I would not have another such dream, though its effect has remained with me to this day, but I did have several other dreams involving Tibor who, each time I had the dream, stood behind me, as a guardian angel might, as if instructing me in Anthroposophy. In the meantime, the dream of Steiner had confirmed my commitment to Anthroposophy for good, whatever the circumstances this commitment would impose upon me in future.

*

As for my relationship to Wenjie: in our partial estrangement from each other, partly from the strict rigors of our study life, partly because we did not share the same social interests in principle (apart from work, society was for her an area where one had "fun" and delighted oneself very simply), but especially because of the fact that we had no sexual relations, we had often between us broached the thought of leaving each other, feeling that the marriage was not meant to be. However, every instance of these discussions only confirmed us in a greater resolve to stay by each other (in almost every instance we both broke down in tears), and, from the strong emotional bond that existed between us, the hope remained that our life together would eventually open up to our mutual satisfaction. Though limited in our lifestyle together, we had been partners in living, had woken up to each other every morning as husband and wife, would spend long hours during the day working together at home on my off-days from teaching, would for the most part eat lunch and supper together, and I was otherwise enamored of her elegant manners and her elegant child-like beauty: in spite of the psychological isolation from which I suffered with her, she was a constant graceful presence. She had also every respect for the creative work I was doing, though she understood nothing of it, not having any intellectual-cultural history in those terms, and she would do everything to ensure that I was free to pursue my work whenever I chose to. She was also inspiring in her ambition about finding a job for herself; with her I felt that the material side of my life would always be addressed and fully secured: nothing would stop her in her resolve to establish us materially. She inspired the sense that something would always happen for us for the better, and she was otherwise altogether faithful in her devotion to her marriage simply as a matter of deep principle.

We were in collusion over her prospects of a work-life in Canada — the goal at which her whole struggle had aimed, and I had been proud of contributing to her success by supporting her over all this time. We were a classic romance: between established westerner and struggling oriental immigrant, and I felt she counted upon me. I was ready to consider the possibility of our moving to Toronto as she hoped we would since she did not feel she could make headway in Montreal without a knowledge of French. A move out of Montreal, which until then had been all my life, represented nothing less than the most painful sacrifice of my life-interests, but I was resolved to allow that Wenjie's interests in *her* young life should have priority over mine, since my own life had by now been lived for the most part. Our chance of moving to Toronto came when I was suddenly offered a Lectureship for three years at the University of Toronto.

The move was made, surprisingly to my great benefit. Learning of my move to Toronto, my publisher, who had himself recently moved there, decided to publish *Othello's Sacrifice* earlier than he had planned, seeing as I could now be counted on to be at the launching to speak about the book, among several other new authors who had their own books to present, to the select few who had been invited. As the book I had written primarily featured Shakespeare and Steiner, I had thought of inviting the Secretary of The Anthroposophical Society in Canada to represent Steiner's Anthroposophy at the launching. In this way, I got to meet Alexandra Barbara Gunther for the first time, and much was to ensue for me from this meeting. With Alexandra, I would go on to found a new Literature and Anthroposophy Group in the Society, from whose discussions numerous significant ideas emerged for me which were to form the basis especially of my writing for the Canadian Society's main journal, *Aurore*, as well as for the Society *Bulletin*. Coming to the Society in Toronto had freed me from the tight hold over the Society maintained by the Quebecois fold of Members in Montreal; I had become free to find myself as an anthroposophist in new terms, untramelled by the network of social interests that had put the Society in Montreal in the hands of the same few over so many years.

My vision of Society activity encompassed the idea of a more broad-minded Membership open to the challenges facing the Society from the outside world. Responding quite spontaneously to ideas recorded in *Aurore* by the Chairman of the Society, I found myself pursuing a line of argument that would engage me in some fresh re-reading of Anthroposophical history as reflected in some of the great art of the Renaissance and post-Renaissance periods. My purpose, as recorded in a series of articles that I was to write for the Society journal, was to show that more would be necessitated from the disposition of the present Society Membership with regard to a full and proper approach to the world at large. The basis for this approach, I argued, was already being suggested to us in the history of the art of those periods, central to the achievement of which was the role of Christian Rosenkreutz, the contours of whose life and influence I had been strenuously researching. At the same time, I suddenly understood more clearly the role I could imagine Christian Rosenkreutz indirectly playing in Shakespeare's own achievement in his late plays, and in this way a third book on Shakespeare was begun.

Amidst this renewed creative upsurge, my married life was, ironically, coming to an end. From her side, Wenjie had been pursuing a direction of life that had been engaging her in many hours of training that kept her away from home continually, and our divergent interests had finally caught up to us. Each of us had found fresh roots and a fresh sense of purpose in this new city, so that it no longer upset us to know that our lives would have to be lived separately. Rather we reflected to each other a sense of excitement about the new prospects that had opened up for each of us separately. I had put it in mind to continue to support Wenjie financially until she'd completed her training as a computer programmer and established herself at a good job. When this was finally achieved, Wenjie set herself up in an apartment in the China-town section of downtown Toronto, on Denison Street just north of Dundas, while I remained behind in our first apart-ment on Isabella Street. In spite of the cheer and the affection-ate respect we maintained about each other through our break up, I told myself this was to be the last time I would go through separation from one I loved. Separation had again been, in another part of me that I had kept to myself, nothing less than heart-wrenching, as well as pathetic in the best and hardest sense of that fine word.

In the company of Wenjie I had known a form of cul-tural innocence that I suspect I would never have gotten to know either in any Western or for that matter any other Oriental context — for I think of this form of innocence as distinctively Chinese. Perhaps it is only made distinctive fi-nally by the addition of fine Chinese women like Wenjie. One might get the feeling of it just from being in that district in Toronto's Chinatown to which Wenjie withdrew when she left. All luxurious excess is cut out of this world, where the most simple human needs are seen to with a committed yet quiet passion. Here too the intellect is kept free, to explore itself at will, if one is in any way inclined to explore oneself creatively. It had been like a return to the simplicity of childhood when one lived unmolested in one's mind, free of the world's war of ambitions, and when one might still be content with the bare peaceful beauty the world afforded. Merely walking along Denison Street up to the baywindow at the street's end, where Wenjie waited looking out for my visit, evoked this world of innocence so strongly in me. Out of this simple context, with which she seemed always to surround herself, Wenjie had appeared — a stunningly beautiful, young Chinese woman, of remarkable intellectual elegance — though this conflux of worlds had been too simply right for someone of my complex kind. Nevertheless, I thought of the struggle of many other young Chinese women of today for whom I reserve a deep admiration, for in their very special innocence (perhaps the last that is left of innocence to humankind) they seem to offer so much fresh hope for our future life in the West. However, from the repressive control that Chinese men continue to exercise over them, it is also clear to me why these remarkable female souls might in the end never inherit the transforming role I could see them having in Western society in future.

*

My Calliope would not spare me with anyone or anything, not even as regards the Anthroposophical Society in which I had hoped to acquire some significant social function. I felt this disappointment in spite of the success I had in getting a number of pieces published in the Society journal and in its bulletin. I discovered that hardly anyone I met seemed ready to pursue shared ideas very far, even when these turned out to be their own ideas further developed. What's more, older personalities, in spite of what struck me as their narrower views, seemed continually to be privileged, to the point of the pre-emption of a new development of ideas. This I learned when my main article on Christian Rosenkreutz was finally published. Though my article speaks in detail of outstanding paintings by Rembrandt which we can only appreciate while we have them before us, the editor had chosen not to reproduce two of the three I address, opting instead to reproduce two paintings around the article by the Society's Chairman, which were by no means indispensable to that article and indeed mere embellishment. With this act of deference, the editors had missed their chance, I thought, of taking the thinking offered through the Society's journal to a more mature level of suffering depth (as I found this illustrated by the paintings in question) beyond the childlike self-absorption that continued to be favored. Ironically, I shared my disillusionment about Society attitudes at this time with Eric, of all people, who wrote back to express his similar view of the Society's group work as too often "a fruitless exchange of set ways of thinking" marked by a "refusal even to contemplate one's deep-rooted fear of change." I had sent Eric a copy of my recent book on Shakespeare and Steiner, and he had responded with enthusiastic approval. My best hopes for the book were confirmed when Eric lent his wholehearted support to my expression of my views in the book. I took encouragement especially from the letters of appreciation about the book that I received from a set of people who, among themselves, reinforced my notion of the possibility of bridging worlds, though for the present I was the only one in whom these worlds had come together.

Confirmation that the book had rigorously achieved its objectives was provided from the anthroposophical side not only by Eric but also by Sergei O. Prokofieff (unquestionably,

the most important anthroposophical writer of our time). He
had also written to me, to say that he thought the book's
argument "very good." From the critical side I heard from my
other Shakespeare mentor at East Anglia, Anthony Gash, who
found my argument especially revealing where I treat of the
import of the history of Shakespeare criticism in this century.
Finally I heard, from the literary side, from the Poet Laureate
himself, the late Ted Hughes, who also had written to say that
he found the book "very interesting stuff," mentioning in his
letter to me that he had some familiarity with Steiner through
a friend who was a nurse at a Steiner clinic, and that he was
eager to see Steiner's plays performed some day. The academic reception in the journals, by comparison, was uneven,
with reviewers (writing prejudicially out of the "post-mod-
ern" scene) already inclined to judge the book before they had
even begun to instruct themselves adequately about the
book's background or the strong lineage I had traced. I was
especially struck by how little understanding remained in the
academic world of a living tradition of Shakespeare criticism
out of the past. The critics who, from the time I first undertook
my research in England, had come off the page for me in the
living glory of their passionate and enlightened prose might
just as well have never lived or written at all, for there had
been no real experience of this criticism from the places where
my book was being reviewed and certainly no sense that I had
offered my book as a continuation of that living tradition. On
the other hand, two strong favorable reviews of my first book
had culminated in a strong appreciative reading of both books
by the reputable editor, Arthur F. Kinney, in *English Language
Notes*. Kinney had finally hit the nail on the head where he
writes of my concern (with Steiner) to seek "to inform the
imagination with cognition" as our only sure way in the end
of confronting the general problem of ego and libido. Kinney,
to whom I had sent the books more recently, had personally

taken up their cause with great ardor and, with his review, had finally justified my work in the academic world.

*

It seems that I had always been meant by my Calliope to be detached from all personal and social relationships for which I might have felt myself meant, and this would also be the case in my all-determining experience of Anthroposophy. Here too I would remain, strictly speaking, *her* "son," which is to say always her *own* "detached" creation, though to what further end I could not begin to divine. I would have to continue to establish my relationship to Anthroposophy strictly out of my own self, without prospect of continued attachments whether to one sphere of society or another, whether in the Society or outside it. The disillusionment I passed through from this overall impasse entailed for me at a certain point a form of separation from the Anthroposophia Being with whom I had sporadically connected over the years. She seemed to me to have walked the earth, along with the Christ Being whom She serves, in that great time when all seemed right with the world, when all great influences that seemed intended to shape me seemed to have converged, namely: Joe and the Church, Marilyn in her own great sphere, as well as Anthroposophy itself, in the days when Tibor was alive. I continued to feel connected with this Anthroposophia Being in a fitful way, right up to that time of intensive study on Milton Street when, as the end point of my study, I had finally come round to addressing the whole value and purpose of the Anthroposophical Society, and especially the great role to be played by Novalis in years to come, as an extension of the work already accomplished by Rudolf Steiner. At this point access to the Society had been closed off to me, ironically by Eric himself. The period that followed may have brought fuller possession of my intellectual resources, on a scale unlike any I had known before, not least in the form of my under-standing of the history that Anthroposophy fulfils, but in the case of service to the Anthroposophia Being there had always been a fine line to walk, where intellect opens out on spiritual being, and that line had momentarily been snapped. In a sense that has seemed to me only too real, this Being has, for the moment, been "returned" to the realm of death and hell out of which at one time in my life She had sprung. In the meantime my intellectual commitment to Anthroposophy continues, though it remains a hard thing to relate myself back properly to the task strenuously set for our time by Steiner, for whom the work of Anthroposophy entailed spe-cifically: comprehending "the spiritual world," not out of personal fantasy or group enthusiasm merely but, directly, out of "the present intellectual standards," standards that ought finally to relate Anthroposophy openly and fully to the world.

*

Left in a new city by now on my own, I found myself growing closer to a young woman of twenty-seven whose appeal to me had, in the meantime, brought me back to the finest points of my childhood when, amidst my place at school, I had contemplated, only from afar, the magical beauty of Irish things. Jennifer O'Connell had been my student in two courses at the University of Toronto before we finally became passionately involved with each other in the late winter of 1998. I had for the longest time kept an immense distance between us, even in our relations as teacher and student, on account of the fierceness of her adherence to the Roman Catholic faith as well as to the Irish Republican cause she had occasionally espoused, to the point I could see of a sort of fanaticism. But I would eventually get to know Jennifer better, as a young woman of profound poetic and religious sensibility, for whom the espousal of fanatical forms of belief was merely a rhetorical parti pris: a boasting of things Irish only because she never had, in her young past, ever intimately shared her deep Irishness with another to the extent she had hoped she could. She had been a regular church-going Catholic for some years, and fittingly our relationship began to develop strongly over the St. Patrick's Day celebrations in the city, two of which we attended that year, the first a preparatory event at St. Cecilia's Church in Downsview, the second at St. Michael's Cathedral in downtown Toronto on the great Feast Day itself.

I was being returned with a vengeance to that part of my cultural past that I had entirely neglected from the time I had stopped performing at the St. Patrick's Day concert with the Holy Family Church Choir in my youth. Certainly by the time I was going to college and I had become immersed in the rigors of academic discipline, I had already lost touch with my own Irishness: a sad commentary, one would think, on the kind of allegiance that I felt the academic world demanded of me. This was with the exception, of course, of the occasion of the Feast Day itself, right up to the time I left home, which my father always had us proudly celebrating, with full shocks of shamrocks provided for all to wear. The homily and general occasion on this latest Feast Day had put me in mind of what little thought I had ever given to that great journey across the ocean that my great-grandfather had once taken, along with so many others many of whom would lose their lives in the attempt, escaping from the worse perils of the Great Famine of that time and the infamy of humiliated dependence on the English. To my great shame, in light of my forgetfulness over all these years, I bore his very name — John O'Meara, though I remembered him only for a worn photograph of him that had been casually nailed to a beam in the backshed of the third-storey apartment that my uncle continued to live in, which had also been my father's home as a child. If anyone would bring me back to a consciousness of the cultural roots I had virtually abandoned, that would be Jennifer, who bore her own Irishness with a constant self-awareness that compared closely with my father's, and indeed in her very appearance she bore an uncanny resemblance to my father's family, especially to my father's sister.

It almost seemed to me as if it were my father who, from the other side of the grave, had led us to each other, and it was uncannily on the very day of his birthday, July 15, that our relationship became as it were personally solemnized between us, when it became clear to us both that we had become emotionally committed to each other and when I remember deliberately choosing to open myself at last to her extraordinary graceful influence. We sat, on that day of the most balmy warmth, on what would become our favorite bench in our favorite haunt at Victoria University Campus in Toronto, in the square just off to the right from the Pratt Library under the inter-tangled boughs of bushes that overhang a long line of benches there, on which no one else would ever sit, at least while we were there. From this spot we commanded a view of the entire grounds that included Victoria Hall and the great green space before us so majestically marked at its center by that great sprawling oak tree around which long tables were sometimes set with great white tablecloths that in the gentle summer wind, as the cloths fluttered, made a profound religious impression as of a church altar: the tables had been set in preparation for a wedding reception of the sort that was occasionally held there. There was also another space just behind the overhanging boughs, where stairs led down to lower grounds in which an inoperative fountain and a garden display were simply placed, and before these we sat on occasion in a still greater seclusion. As we sat tucked away in this spot unknown to anyone, I would recite to this dear "daughter of the swan" the Yeats she now revered as the greatest poet, whose work I had introduced her to as her teacher, and here too I would sing to her her favorite song, the "Moonlight in Mayo," which she had introduced to me. We had made, in this way, this hallowed place our own, and to this day our very souls and selves remain written all over those gracious grounds.

I recall our going up, towards the middle of summer, to Wasaga Beach on what seemed an inauspicious day of lowering clouds, so that the crowds were down, and the day suddenly turned splendid, almost as soon as we arrived. We lay ourselves down in the sudden sun and read lazily. I had gone back to reading some of the literature of the past in the light of the vision Anthroposophy offers of the great Indian, Hebrew and Greek cultural lines in their long progression towards the central Christ-event, and I had reached the point of turning to the Greeks and to Homer. I was by then immersed in a reading once again of the *Iliad* and of the *Odyssey*, all of which got intermixed at the time in my imagination of the moment and the place where we lay stretched out. A great resort center in the far distance from where we sat, as the Bay curved to our left, looked like it might be the great tower of Illium, and when Jennifer took to the water to wade through it momentarily, it seemed to me as if I might be looking on the resplendent figure of Nausicaa herself in the all-redeeming freshness of her youth. In another pose and another moment she had turned herself into Pallas Athena who was now sternly dictating fresh hope to me after a long, overworn life in which I had felt continually adrift. From Jennifer I learned that O'Meara and O'Connell were among the very oldest clans from ancient Ireland, and I had fancifully imagined Meara, or as it was originally known Meadhra (pronounced

Mara), as a clan especially remembered for coming over from across the sea (perhaps from Atlantis itself) and Connell as the clan remembered for its association with the rocky coastline against which we had abutted. Jennifer and I also learned that propagation between these two clans today represented a great thing in relation to that ancient past in which they had kept scrupulously separate. However that may be, by October of 1998, Jennifer had indeed become pregnant with our child, and I will never forget that day one late Friday afternoon in late October when we stood in my office at Erindale College Rm 294B, looking out from the high narrow window behind my desk to discover in the bluebeech tree that stood there (no more than ten feet away) a cardinal, in sumptuous red, who had suddenly arrived, continually re-positioning itself among its branches, hiding away among the long leaves that had all turned yellow, so that our vision of the bird was difficult in every moment. We had had to work at re-locating it every time it re-positioned itself, and, having found it, we had had to fix upon it carefully or else we would lose sight of it again. Two weeks later, in early November, it re-appeared to us once again on a Friday, this time in a tree that by then had lost all its leaves, so that the bird could now be seen without obstruction. That morning there had been light snow.

Just over two weeks after that, Jennifer and I made a visit to the radioscopy clinic for an ultra-sound on the baby, only to discover the tragic news that the foetus had stopped growing. No heart beat could be found, though from its condition they could tell that the foetus had stopped growing about a week to ten days before that. We had learned of this in the morning, had travelled over to Jennifer's family doctor for further advice, and Jennifer had taken the decision with her doctor to have the D and C that very day. It was to be an exhausting, not to say a humiliating, affair, to think only of the long wait we had at the hospital and the ill-mannered treatment we received from hospital attendants. When they finally released Jennifer from hospital, it was three o'clock in the morning. It had been by far the most tiring day I have ever been through, not to think of what Jennifer had been through, which afflicted me to the point of an intolerable sadness, and it would take us many, many days to recover from the trauma. To return to the home, which we had hitherto filled with the warm thought of the child that was coming to us, was among the bleakest experiences I have known, and the following morning, as Jennifer slept on, I could not contain my tears which streamed with the sense of the loss of our own that I now felt all too keenly.

And now as I write, some four months later, I once again face the prospect of another tenure at university coming to an end. By the end of April, I will be seeking for new work again, as my tenure at the University of Toronto expires. Once again I face the humiliating challenge of seeking work among Canadian universities and university colleges that have already written back to thank me for my interest, a sign that I am not the kind of candidate they are seeking. Ten years of continuous teaching at university (including teaching almost every summer) across a very broad spectrum of courses to very many students, as well as my success in writing two books that between them have garnered nine reviews in my field — all this is not enough, and never will be, to impress the hiring committees who are only looking to fill their own needs from some remote office where innumerable applications lie stacked before them. It used to be that one could find work through the souls one met — souls who would have learned, in meeting you, of the work that you could do. In the meantime, I must hope that some unforeseen need will make my services suddenly wanted somewhere, though I cannot be sure that this random fate will be bestowed on me again. I look out once again on the bluebeech tree that stands outside my office window, at its bare winter beauty (so astonishingly variegated and living yet, the bare forms of trees in winter), as Jennifer works on at her term paper in her own corner of the office at the other desk that she has made her own, and my thoughts fix once again on the idea that she might be carrying our child. St. Patrick's Day is only two days away. I turn back to my desk to address the term papers that continue to require my attention, but I find that I cannot for the moment drive away from my thoughts the words of the song of "Mayo" to which my mind has strayed, and at a certain point it seems to me that this song is streaming to me once again as from an other shore:

> Her Irish eyes like beacons shine all through
>   the darkest night.
> I know their sweet love beams will always fill
>   the world with light.
> The roses of her cheeks will lend enchantment to the sea,
> And when the shamrocks wear the dew I'll wed
>   my sweet Coleen.
>
> For her Irish eyes are smiling,
> And an Irish heart is pining,
> When I kissed her and caressed her
> In the gloaming long ago . . .
>
> Irish arms will hold and press you,
> And an Irish heart caress you,
> And her Irish lips will bless you
> In the moonlight in Mayo.
>
> And her Irish lips will bless you
> In the moonlight in Mayo.

March 15, 1999